PRISON IS MY PARISH

The Story of Park Tucker

PRISON IS MY PARISH

The Story of **PARK TUCKER**
as told to George Burnham

FLEMING H. REVELL COMPANY

LIBRARY OF CONGRESS CATALOG CARD NUMBER: 57-9963

1.4

Westwood, New Jersey
London E.C.4—29 Ludgate Hill
Glasgow C.2—229 Bothwell Street

DEDICATION

THIS BOOK IS dedicated to a loving and merciful God, who gave me life when I deserved death in the bowels of the earth. I also dedicate it to Margaret, my dear wife, and our children, Lynelle Dixon and Richard Park. Grateful appreciation is given to Mr. James V. Bennett and the men of the Bureau of Prisons, Warden F. T. Wilkinson, the staff and the members of our church at Atlanta.

H. PARK TUCKER

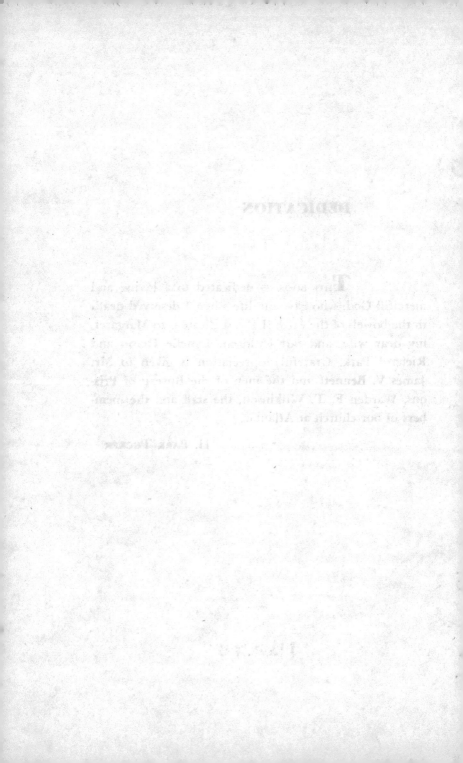

CONTENTS

INTRODUCTION

Every once in a while a book is published which combines in its appeal a document of human interest and a commentary on our social institutions. This story of Chaplain Tucker is such a book. His successful attempt to raise himself above the economic level into which he was born is not in itself uncommon in our American life, but the quality of a simple religious faith that dominates the book makes the story worth the telling.

The other appeal this book has lies in the fact that Reverend Tucker writes from the vantage point of a prison chaplain. To most people, the prison still symbolizes society's demand for retribution and punishment of the offender. Yet throughout the history of prisons, the chaplain has been the chief contender for more constructive policies and programs within the prison, and as a representative of the church he personifies the redemptive philosophy of religion for all men.

INTRODUCTION

The importance of religion, religious education, and spiritual counseling for men in prison is beyond debate, and the value of a chaplain in the prison setting needs no defense. What we do need, however, is a deeper and more sympathetic understanding of the man in prison and his problems, as well as a sincere willingness to assist him in finding his proper place when he returns, as he must, to our communities. To this end, Chaplain Tucker has made a worthwhile contribution. For this as well as for its inspirational value the book deserves a warm welcome.

JAMES V. BENNETT, *Director*
U. S. Bureau of Prisons

FOREWORD

FOREWORD

BY ALL THE laws of man, I should be dead.
I live by the graciousness and mercy of God. Like Paul,
I pen an epistle to the people from my private prison
here in Atlanta, Georgia.

Years ago, as an ignorant coal miner, number 602,
I was being crushed to death in the aftermath of a mine
explosion when God saved my life and my soul. Now,
years later, I sit in the office of the Protestant Chaplain
at the Atlanta Federal Penitentiary, endeavoring to
point other men to their own Saviour, Christ the Lord.
Surely this book and my writing is an act similar to the
one Paul speaks of in his epistle to the church at Cor-
inth: "Therefore if any man (even miner 602) be in
Christ, he is a new creature: old things are passed away;
behold, all things are become new."

This book is a culmination of the efforts of many
people who have "stooped to lift me up." It is stated
that "no man ever stands so straight as he who stoops to
help a boy." I think of the many who have helped me;

11

the men who rescued me, the doctor and nurses who helped me gain my health; Rev. Henry Corey; my father, mother, and sisters; the teachers at Wheaton Academy, Houghton College, Eastern Seminary, and many others.

Every word, sentence, illustration and story in this book have been prayed about, and have been enacted in love, tragedy, and with God's forgiveness. May this narrative be a projection of your own life and the men living and dead who have caused you to be the person you are in God's love.

It is my desire that this book will be a blessing to your soul, bring stability to your life, and re-dedication to Christ and His Kingdom.

H. PARK TUCKER, *Chaplain*

U. S. Penitentiary
Atlanta, Georgia

PRISON IS MY PARISH

The Story of Park Tucker

IN THE BEGINNING

OVER A HUNDRED people had gathered at the prison entrance.

A grin spread over my face as I warmed inside to think they had taken the trouble to meet me. I couldn't quite understand why I warranted such a reception. Maybe my reputation as a tough coal miner and seat-of-the-pants flier had gone on ahead.

I had landed my plane on a bumpy farm the day before near Kennesaw Mountain, but such landings were nothing for people to get excited about. I had done it lots of times.

An officer came over as I approached the gate. He told me I would have to step around to the side.

"What's going on?" I asked.

"This is the committee that is saying goodbye to Warden Joseph Sanford, who is leaving to be head of the correctional department for the State of Michigan."

Such was my humbling introduction to the big house—officially known as the United States Penitentiary in Atlanta, Georgia.

I stood off to the side and looked at the vastness of the prison. It made me feel small, in spite of two hundred pounds spread over a six-foot two-inch frame.

My eyes moved slowly from the rugged gate to the high walls. The prison looked strong. And it was. It sat on the granite roots of Stone Mountain, the largest exposed rock in the Western Hemisphere. The veins of granite had yielded stones to build locks of the Panama Canal, the dome of the gold repository at Fort Knox and steps of the east wing of the United States Capitol Building in Washington, D. C. De Soto was said to have been the first white man to lay eyes upon the mountain. He named it the New Gibraltar, a name that stuck for many years.

Granite from the mountain had gone into the prison buildings and the cell houses. Thousands of tons of concrete made the wall thirty-seven feet high—four feet thick at the ground and two feet wide at the top. Seven years in the building, the wall enclosed twenty-seven acres.

It was difficult to imagine anyone, no matter how desperate, scaling such walls. But they had been scaled by men seeking freedom.

My thoughts raced back over the life that had led me to the place where I now stood. And I thought about the thousands of other men who had stood near the same spot since the first group of inmates had shuffled into the prison on January 20, 1902.

The average sentence of the men was seven years. I was in for life, and wanted it that way. I was the new prison chaplain. My life had been dedicated to God when a miracle occurred during a coal mine explosion. I wanted to help the men find a better way.

[I wasn't sure that I was prepared for the difficulties and opportunities that lay behind the walls. There were about 2,600 men inside. They had committed crimes and were separated from society. The fragile thread of their normal lives with wives, children and girl friends had been snapped by policemen, judges and indignant citizens.]

No preacher ever had a stranger congregation. The men had come from forty-eight states, three outlying possessions and sixteen foreign countries—the biggest international outfit in the world with the exception of the United Nations.

There were 171 Army prisoners, five Navy prisoners and no Marines. There were 1,788 whites, 768 Negroes, three Indians and no Chinese. There were 2,559 men and no women. There were many lifers and one man with ninety-nine years. Another man had a sentence of life and five years, which in my opinion constituted an unconstitutional infringement by the judge on eternity.

There were 721 in the prison for stealing cars. Second place went to the narcotic offenders, with 257, not counting marijuana. Bringing up the rear were those sentenced for income tax evasion, cattle rustling, train wrecking, bank robbery and violation of the Mann Act.

If one man had to serve all the time on the books it would take him 19,027½ years. If he had started at the birth of Christ he would have finished only about a tenth of it and would not be eligible for parole until four thousand more years passed.

The penitentiary has housed some of the most infamous men in the annals of crime—a member of the "Rat Gang" from St. Louis, a former governor, one connected with the Crown Jewels overseas during World War II, another who tried to assassinate President Truman, and Puerto Rican Nationalists who shot up Congress in 1954.

Al Capone, Chicago gang leader, had served time for income tax evasion before his death. One inmate was a bona fide candidate for the Presidency of the United States. He was Eugene V. Debs, the perennial Socialist candidate. Debs arrived at the pen seven months after the World War I armistice was signed to serve ten years for making speeches that allegedly interfered with the war effort. But prison life did little to daunt him.

To accept his nomination, he was allowed to go to the front steps of the prison, where newsreel men, photographers and reporters were waiting. Almost a hundred of his Socialist supporters thronged the sidewalk.

Newspapers reported that James M. Cox (a Democratic opponent) was going to make his speeches from the rear of a train and that Debs would make his from a cell. After reading this, Debs sent off a note to the papers saying that at least the voters would know where he stood.

His campaign statements were limited by the officials to five hundred words.

Some of the prisoners were misled by the prominence given his picture and statements in the national press. They thought he would be elected and rejoiced over the sweeping prison reforms he would execute.

Warren G. Harding and the Republicans won in a landslide. But Debs received nearly one million votes. Shortly afterwards, he was pardoned by President Harding.

I knew that I had to know something about these men, their thought processes and dreams of the future, if I planned to be more than a name on a door. And I was determined not to be a prison chaplain who just went through the motions. Prison chaplains usually have three strikes on them before they go to bat. I was going down swinging, if I had to go down.

An inmate editor had described it this way:

"From the inmate angle, the chaplain has been either a somewhat emasculated screw, a medium for the shooting of angles, or a pious bore. From the official standpoint, the chaplain has been either (and sometimes simultaneously) a seeker of favors, an interferer with custody or a pious bore. Mild contempt was his due from both groups."

One of the first things I did after getting inside was to throw my shoulders back and walk around the mess hall, speaking to the men. I wanted them to know that I was proud of my position. Several of them told me later they thought I was the new warden. It seemed that "Holy Joes" were not in the habit of mingling with the men outside of the office.

The men may have been impressed by the fact that I was larger than most of them, and that none of it was fat, thanks to long years of hard work. They looked me over closely, with searching eyes. None noticed that the left hand dangling from my sleeve was rigid. An expert attempt had been made to duplicate the human hand, with flesh and blood tint, after the arm had been mangled in an accident years before.

I had never been a prisoner. I wanted to know all I could about the thoughts behind the faces. One of them helped set me straight:

"It is difficult for a man to envision the reality of prison before entering its gates. He thinks of it in terms of the physical: separation from loved ones, sexual abstinence, possible brutality, his age upon release and its effects on his way of life. If his sentence is fifteen years, he finds it dreamlike, unreal, for he doesn't seem to be able to picture himself fifteen years hence. He can't plan what he will do when he leaves prison for he can't imagine what changes fifteen years will have wrought in himself and his environment. Will there still be jobs available in his trade? Will there be a depression? Who will be living and who dead? Will there be a home left to which to return? How will he feel after ten or fifteen years? All these questions are raised in the mind of the man waiting to enter a prison's gates; but only time can answer them, so the inmate thinks of the immediate future and its physical reality.

'The decline of human dignity will begin within a few hours of his prison arrival. All his personal belongings will be taken from him to be locked away until his release. He will be stripped, prodded, probed, the orifices of his body inspected for contraband—this in the name of custody or security, words that he will come to dread through the years.

'His first twenty-four hours in the prison will probably be his hardest. He has seen the grim walls, the towering tiers of cells, the uniformed guards, the prisoners passing silently in the corridors. He has not been cuffed, sworn at nor harshly treated. But he has felt a weight added to his shoulders, a tightening of the skull, a heaviness in the air that he can't define.

"The smallness and the solitude of the quarantine cell squeezes thought from him. The life he has so recently left behind becomes sharply etched, so real that he can see it, smell it, hear the echo of voices that he may never really hear again. In that first twenty-four hours he knows more loneliness, more hopelessness, more anguish and more remorse than he has ever known before or than he may ever know again.

"In the days that follow he is caught up in the new routine, and his loneliness abates. There is much to learn, many stories to hear, new sounds, new sights. He is drawn out of himself and begins to see the need to plan at least his near future, his institution life. He reaches a decision on how he will do his time to best advantage.

"There are many roads open to him. Some men do all their time the hard way, perpetually flouting authority. Others simply work and listen to the radio-phones —nothing more. Some read continually. Others play— in the cell, the mess hall, at work; they scuffle, punch, guffaw. There is the cult of Atlas, dedicated to the body beautiful; the intellectuals, frowning disdainfully on all but their own small clique; the politicians, pressed, shined, cigarred; the gamblers, with their pools, bets and loans, who seem immune to their steady diet of punitive segregation. There are the wise and the mentally deficient, the kind and the sadistic, the clean and the filthy. A man finds that he must live with all these in peace and harmony and that dire consequences await those who cannot acclimate themselves. (Gamblers, welchers and stool pigeons are separated by an inner prison to keep them from being killed.)

"There are eight men in his cell, seven besides himself. Just being in that cell exerts a steady pressure. It is not the bars nor the narrowness of his space. It is

22

this heterogeneous humanity demanding his conforma-
tion. The man above him is illiterate, loud; the man
beside him is undoubtedly homosexual. Above him is a
man who never speaks to anyone. On the other side of
the cell are two buddies who spend their time plotting
new crimes. Of the other two, one is an old man who
has spent forty years in many prisons and the other is
a kid of twenty who wears his shirt collar turned up
and acts tough to hide his fears. The old man is the best
of the lot; he has learned how to live and let live in this
morass.

"The one thing that the man comes to live with
which causes him the most anguish is the complete lack
of privacy. He may spend years within the walls without ever having the revitalizing experience of a single
quarter-hour of meditative solitude, away from prying
eyes, distracting sounds or sights. He performs the
most personal of human offices in a crowded cell; he
bathes hurriedly, twice weekly, in a mob of shouting,
surging nakedness. These are realities of imprisonment
that he cannot escape, that he learns to live with."

Another clean-cut young man, who would have
looked at home on any college campus if he hadn't
attempted to be another second-story Raffles, expressed
similar thoughts and experiences:

"Twenty-five tired and hungry prisoners emerged
from the bus and marched up the stone steps and through
the massive prison gates. I was one of them.

"It was then that a terrifying thought struck me. Hard
and sickening. This is where I would spend the best part

of the next twenty years. Fear slowly began to creep over me. I'm sure that others have experienced the same feeling. No doubt some of them would deny they ever felt this fear. I'm not sure. I only know I felt it.

"Prison itself was not something new to me. My thoughts raced back to my last prison experience—the time I had served a five-year sentence on a chain gang. A chain gang was prison. This was prison. All the bitter memories of that hell-on-earth began to bounce around in my brain again. Twelve hours of back-breaking labor a day. A diet of corn bread and beans. The sweltering heat. The sweat boxes. Ignorant guards. The leg chains. The whip. The shotguns. Sadistic punishments like working in filth and muck and being forced to drink large cups of castor oil.

"The word is still fear. Not a trembling fear, but the kind that would make you fight like a madman if you were backed into a corner.

"The front gates of the prison clanged shut. We were inside now. I looked around. This was the Administration Building. It was large, clean, well lighted, marble floors, almost like the entrance to any office building— except for the bars on the windows. I wondered what lay beyond the almost pleasant surroundings of this building . . . out there . . . in the cell blocks.

"Then came the first unexpected surprise. A voice broke the silence. A kindly, pleasant, soft voice. 'We know that you men are tired and hungry after the long ride here, but be patient. We'll see that you are taken care of as soon as possible.'

"I looked around for the owner of the voice. He was one of the officials. I eyed him suspiciously. I expected his voice to explode any moment. But nothing happened.

"That seemed to be the beginning—the beginning of a long series of events that would help to quell the fear and turmoil that were tearing me apart inside; the beginning of things that were to help me subdue my bitterness and self-conflicts and, worst of all, the crushing memories."

THE PALACE

THE FEDERAL PEN, known by the inmates as "the palace on McDonough Boulevard," has a personality all its own. The men are tough—but they can laugh—some of the loudest chuckles come at the movies, when Humphrey Bogart talks out of the side of his mouth.

This sense of humor is a great stabilizing force. The men get big laughs from the people who brag about being able to tell a criminal by his face. On the bulletin board are several pictures. Visitors are asked to pick out the criminal. Invariably they will select an officer who looks like a bank robber, and the chaplain, who has the earmarks of being a hired gunman.

A former chaplain lived a hard life at Atlanta, because he failed to realize the men were still human beings. He had a heart of suspicion instead of compassion and would harangue them at every opportunity.

The laundry detail retaliated by pressing his pants on the side, like bellbottom sailor trousers. He thought it odd, but figured it was some kind of prison regulation.

His sermons were filled with flowery statements, like "let me take you to the mountain tops." And the inmate church population would audibly reply: "Go ahead, we'd love to go."

The men, however, can laugh just as heartily at themselves. Shortly after having all his teeth pulled, a man went to the commissary. He had only two dollars and told the officer to give him two dollars worth of anything. The officer gave him a dollar's worth of chewing gum and a dollar's worth of toothpaste.

Another inmate was caught with ten pieces of ham he had stolen from the mess hall. He wasn't very upset at being caught with the stolen goods, or with the discipline that would follow. He was humiliated because his friends would know he had been eating ham. He was a Jew.

The prisoners are ingenious.

A man wanted a clock and couldn't afford to buy one. He found a piece of cardboard, printed the numbers and painted it prettily. Hands and gears were made from old parts. A spring and other essentials weren't available, but a steady source of power was found. He placed the clock in front of the cell's ventilation system.

The exhaust kept the timepiece running, without winding.

A prisoner named Jack found a way to beat the summer heat. While working on other pipes at his assignment in the plumbing shop, he managed to install a private line to his cell from the ice water supply. He used almost enough pipe for a junior Texas oil well and cooled off in comfort. Officers might not have discovered the contraption if a fellow inmate "next door" hadn't "ratted" on Jack because he wouldn't add an extension.

It was rumored that men in the power house had contraband food at night. The area was kept under surveillance. One day an officer saw a small string alongside one of the tanks. This brought out a heavier string. Then came a rope. Tied on the end of the rope was a large milk can, which contained bread, cheese, ham and all the fixings. Prisoners mourned the loss of their milk-can commissary.

When this was discovered, a prisoner found another way to enjoy a late snack fit for a king. Pigeons were plentiful around the institution yards. He caught a squab and dressed it. Onions, potatoes, and seasoning were added. The only legitimate ingredient was peppers he had raised in the garden. Then came the problem of how to cook it. He obtained some cardboard, which gives off a lot of heat without much smell or smoke. All the ingredients were placed in a can. Five strips of cardboard later, he had a delicious stew.

An inmate cocktail was made by dissolving a Milky Way candy bar in a glass of hot water.

Boredom is one of the biggest problems faced by the men. Thrown together into an unwilling society, they often get on each other's nerves and violent tragedy results.

Bad blood was discovered between two inmates. Finally the story came out. One of them had bought a 1945 Packard from the other. The buyer took his family for a ride up into the hills. He noticed that the car had difficulty pulling the grades and finally came to one that it couldn't make. He lifted the hood and found a 1935 Ford engine.

Both men were car thieves.

Inmates have their own code for evaluating people. A truckload of peaches was stolen from the institution orchard. Prisoners had put in long hours of work there.

"He's the worst crook I've ever known," commented one.

A popular drink at "The Palace" during the warm months, when more fortunate people are vacationing at the mountains or seashore, is one made from fruit mints, in several flavors. The ingredients—a little hot water to melt it, plus ice water. Not many bars serve such a variety of drinks for a nickel.

The easiest crime ever solved at the pen concerned the fellow who stole some sugar from the mess hall. He put the sugar in an envelope and tied it to his leg. As he walked down the long corridor, the envelope split a little and a small stream of sugar poured out onto the floor, leaving a telltale trail up the corridor, into the cell block, up the stairs and down the range to the cell door. He entered the cell, reached down to remove the prize, found the empty envelope, turned his head and saw the last few grains outside the door. In the midst of the grains was an officer's foot. The prisoner's eyes traveled slowly upwards and his face was beet red by the time the face was reached.

Such petty thefts are a minor problem. Plans for release are something else. The day never sets in a penitentiary that someone isn't dreaming and scheming on ways to get out.

Whenever I hear that an escape has been effected, I immediately leave the prison and go home. If the prisoners ever thought for a minute that I was involved in plans to recapture them my work as a chaplain would be finished. They would never again believe I am there to help them.

One of the most spectacular escapes involved two men I will call Smith and Hodges. It was decided that Smith would saw one of the bars in the mop room on the second floor of the hospital. Hodges would be the lookout. A tubercular patient, he was to cough if anyone came in sight. The bar was almost out when Smith heard the cough. He came out of the mop room and ran into an attendant. Both men overpowered him and finished cutting the bar. They lowered themselves to the ground on sheets tied together. Still inside the prison proper, they took advantage of darkness to approach the walls and then dug up a rope ladder they had buried beforehand. The ladder was connected to Tower No. 5, which was not in use at the time.

They rode a streetcar to the heart of Atlanta and then took a cab to the nearby suburb of Decatur. There they caught a freight train to Madison County, only to be overtaken by a posse.

Hodges surrendered and was returned to the prison. Smith resisted. He was shot three times and taken to a hospital in Athens, Georgia. When the guard had to leave the room for a moment, he escaped again. The countryside was alerted. One of the prison officers, however, figured Smith was too badly hurt to leave the hospital. Accompanied by a nurse, he began a search of the premises. In the basement they found a pile of clothing. The officer pulled his pistol and shouted: "All right, Smith, come out." The clothes began to move and out came Smith, pleading, "Mr. Williams, don't shoot. You know me."

The nurse fainted. While the officer's attention was diverted by this, Smith climbed through a window and escaped again.

He was later apprehended in Muncie, Indiana, but not before he had committed a series of crimes. He requested that he be allowed to return to Atlanta, but was handed over to Connecticut authorities for murder. Hanging was his last escape.

Inmates were presented red and white roses by visiting church women at a Mother's Day service one year. A prisoner escaped by dressing in women's clothes and going out with the visiting mothers. His capture was swift.

Two men made good another escape by tunneling

under the wall between Towers No. 6 and 7. At that time a tuberculosis camp was located near the section of wall and the tunneling was done from under the floor of a tent. The dirt was disposed of by using it atop the terraces in the camp area.

After many months of patient digging in the narrow space, both squeezed through the tunnel to freedom. One was later captured. The other was killed in a gun battle at Muskegon, Michigan.

Two other prisoners, who were serving time for bank robbery, noticed a storm sewer near the handball courts and often wondered about the location of the exit. They secretly began to explore the sewer.

One day both men squeezed into the sewer, went straight down for about twenty feet and then began to inch their way to freedom. They almost suffocated in the narrow fifteen-inch pipe, but made it. The opening was in a small patch of woods, well hidden from the officer on watch.

They were reported missing at the 5 P.M. count. At first it was believed they might be hiding somewhere within the walls, as two other prisoners had done a year previously. The institution was searched repeatedly from one end to the other. All known exits and possible exits were checked and double-checked, but still there was no clue as to how the men had escaped. Two days later it was still unknown how the men had gotten out.

The warden received a tip on the third day that two more men had escaped, or were escaping, via a storm sewer near the handball courts. The sewer exit out-

THE U.S. PENTENTIARY AT ATLANTA, AS IT LOOKS FROM CHAPLAIN TUCKER'S PLANE.

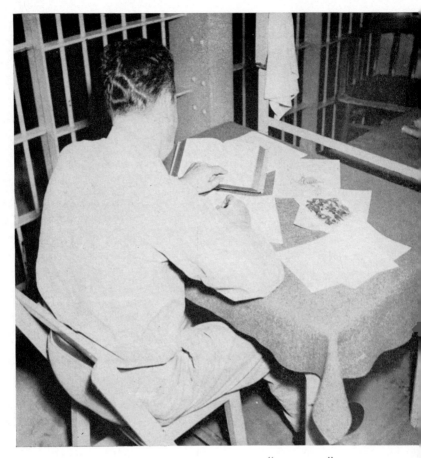

AN INMATE PASSES UP RECREATION IN "THE YARD" TO STUDY
FOR AN EXAM IN THE SELF-STUDY BIBLE COURSE.

side the walls was quickly located. A cordon of heavily-armed officers, FBI agents and local law enforcement men surrounded the area. Within a matter of hours the officers, assisted by bloodhounds, flushed both men from their hiding places in the bushes.

The search for the first two was broadened and intensified throughout a fifteen-state area. Two days later, state patrolmen found a car abandoned near Buchanan, Georgia. This car had been stolen from a location near the institution about the time the pair escaped. FBI agents and Federal prison officials were immediately ordered into the area. One of the men was captured that night in an abandoned house near a swamp. The other, with bloodhounds snapping at his heels, was caught in the swamp next day.

Prisoners could have been escaping through the sewer for years if they had known it was wide enough. At the point where it went beneath the wall there was an iron grill. The first two men cut this on the way out, making it easier for anyone who wanted to follow them.

This escape hatch was plugged up in short order.

A few weeks after the escape episode, the warden attended an inmate variety show. One of the acts went something like this:

First inmate—"Where's Captain Jones?"

Second inmate—"He went to play golf with the warden."

First inmate—"How many holes are they going to play?"

Second inmate—"Oh, about nine holes."

First inmate—"When do you think they'll be back?"

Second inmate—"Oh, in about a month."

First inmate—"How come a month?"

Second inmate—"Well, it took them three days to find *one* hole."

The warden laughed as heartily as anyone else.

HE DIED A FREE MAN

THE ATLANTA PEN, in many ways, can be pictured as a typical American community—with its power plant, large industries, laundry, library, maintenance shops, farms, dairy, kitchens, dining rooms, bakery, schools, hospital, business offices, recreation area, chapels, living quarters, shoe repair shop and garages.

Mailbags used by the U.S. Post Office are products of the huge textile mill. Salaries average about twenty dollars a month.

The game of baseball is played the same as on the outside, with one exception. Every time a ball is fouled over the fence, hundreds of men stand and yell: "Let me go after it, warden."

More than seven thousand meals are served daily in the dining room. Menus are carefully prepared, because a well-fed man isn't as likely to become mutinous. But there is no pampering.

Much of the food comes from two prison farms. One, adjoining the main institution, is used for the production of fruit and smaller garden vegetables. More extensive farming operations are carried on at the Honor Farm of more than fifteen hundred acres, located about eleven miles from the prison.

Inmates form many clubs. There is a town hall forum and an organization of Alcoholics Anonymous. Scores of checker games, with the usual kibitzers, dot the recreational area during free periods. The men have figured out an uncanny number of ways to gamble on checkers, and pity the poor welcher who fails to pay off.

A legend at the institution is "the parole tree." Years ago, when the treeless tuberculosis camp was situated in what is now the recreation area, Mrs. Emma Neal Douglas, a visitor, saw the patients sitting on the shady side of their tents in the bleak compound. She donated six saplings. Only one survived. It was reported that three hundred men could sit under its great shade at one time. They talked and dreamed about parole.

When the area was cleared in 1938 and the great tree fell under the axe, an inmate wrote an article which said:

"Cut down, did I say? No! It was assassinated, lynched, if you will, by a mob of young men and an officer who was told to improve the yard. They had to get the year-and-a-day men to do it. No old timer would be guilty of such an act."

Just beyond the railroad tracks in the rear of the prison, under the great oak trees, was "Boot Hill," a name given by the men to the prison cemetery. Over 150 graves were there.

The yard was clean. Markers, made by the prisoners, bore the name, age, date of death and abbreviation of the state from which the man was sent to prison. Inmates displayed a tender sympathy in the making of markers, for among prisoners there was a common terror of dying in prison.

A traditional story, containing more truth than fiction, has been told about "Boot Hill." It unfolded like this:

Two persons met briefly in one of the Pullman cars of the northbound Crescent Limited, speeding toward Atlanta. One was a Georgia girl, a freshman at the University of Florida who radiated a glow of happiness over her first homecoming. The other was John Williams, a tall, wide-shouldered man, whose lean face was etched with grief as he looked out at an April day. Williams was enroute to New York City, where his mother was seriously ill.

He was checking a timetable, to determine the time of his arrival in New York, when the young girl erupted from her seat and bounced across the aisle. She stood beside him, balancing against the sway and jerks of the train as it slowed on the outskirts of Atlanta. She pointed out the window and exclaimed, excitedly, "There's my home." Then her voice sobered as she added, "And there's my father."

Williams stared out the window at a huge grey wall embracing a number of large stone buildings. Nearby was a cemetery and he saw a large monument which read, "And in Eternal Peace Thy Penance Ends." A small group of people were gathered about an open grave.

He asked, "Where is your father?"

She replied, "One of the inmates must have died. Father is conducting the service. He is chaplain at the Federal Prison."

John Williams was still staring moodily out of the window when the girl left the train at Atlanta. He was searching the labyrinth of memory for images of his own father, a father who had disappeared almost twenty years before.

His mother had cried for a few days and then had gone about the difficult task of caring for him, his brother and sister. She had always evaded their questions as to his father's whereabouts.

When the train arrived in New York, Williams had forgotten about the girl and the prison. He taxied to the hospital and went immediately to his mother's room. His brother and sister welcomed him silently. He stood beside the bed looking down at his mother's beloved face. She lifted her eyes to his, and her lips moved, but she could not speak. She raised a thin hand slowly and pointed to a cabinet sitting beside the bed.

John opened the drawer. He saw a single page, a letter damp with tears. He handed it to his mother and she crumpled it in her hand with the last of her waning strength and dropped it on the floor. John picked it up and put it into his pocket.

Three days later, after the funeral, he noticed the wrinkled letter. He unfolded it and stared with shocked amazement at the letterhead—April 12, 1918, United States Penitentiary, Atlanta, Georgia. The letter read:

"I regret to inform you that your husband, Charles Williams, died in the prison hospital of cancer April 12. Funeral services were held for him the following day.

"As you know, Mr. Williams was released from this institution three years ago, but because of his illness, his shame over his crime, and his fear that returning home might reflect upon his children, he asked to remain at the prison. The request was granted.

"He died a free man."

John Williams stumbled over to the window and looked out upon the busy street. He remembered another window of a few days past—the train window through which he had looked at a cemetery and a newly-made grave—a window through which he had unknowingly observed the burial of his father.

PLAIN TALK IN CHURCH

MY FIRST LOOK at the prison auditorium where I was to hold services was depressing. The room was spacious enough, but it just didn't look like a church. There wasn't much of a church atmosphere.

I realized that the auditorium had to be used for such things as movies and stage presentations, but I was determined there would be a church set-up so the men would have a place for worship.

One of the prisoners agreed to make some church furnishings for me, but had it only half finished when he was paroled. It looked as if the furnishings were going to be a wistful dream, but the prisoner committed another crime in a short time and came back again. I was sorry to see the man return, but lost no time in getting him to complete his project.

I wish I could have had the furnishings the first Sunday that I faced the men as their chaplain. Men and women of great renown had occupied the same stage. There had been Presidents of the United States, organizations such as John Philip Sousa's Band, the great Enrico Caruso, Evangelist Billy Sunday and his famed song leader, Homer Rodeheaver.

The auditorium had seats for 1,650 men, but only a handful were present for my first sermon. Mandatory attendance of church services had been stopped some time before. Most of the men were more interested in playing checkers and dreaming of parole.

For the next few weeks the small crowd remained about the same. After thinking and praying about it, I decided to use the shock treatment. It could have been described as a dirty trick.

I began the Sunday morning talk by asking several questions:

"How many of you men have read the books of the Old Testament?"

Several raised their hands.

"How many have read the books of the New Testament?"

A number of hands went up.

"More specifically, how many of you have read Matthew, Mark, Luke and John?"

Again the hands went up—psychologically, they wanted to be on my side.

"Now I am going to give you a test on the Old Testament. How many have read Genesis, Exodus, Leviticus, Numbers and Deuteronomy?"

About the same number of hands shot skyward.

"This is the final question. How many have ever studied the book of Hezekiah?"

A large portion of the small gathering raised hands.

"Gentlemen," I continued, "I had intended to bring a message this morning on faith from the eleventh chapter of Hebrews, but I have changed my mind. I am going to preach on a text entitled 'The Liar,' and I would like to dedicate it to all of you men who have lied to me and to yourselves.

"There is no book of Hezekiah in the Old Testament."

They sat up straight and listened, as I tried to show them the jeopardy of kidding themselves by being deceitful about the Bible and the things of God. It was a straight talk, as plain as I knew how to give it.

At the conclusion, I told the men I would take the time to write an understandable self-study Bible course if they would cooperate. A number of hands were raised.

The task of compiling such a course for the specific use of prisoners was harder than I had anticipated. Maps, charts and graphs were used.

And it wasn't any easier on the men who volunteered. They went back to their cells and told their buddies about the shock treatment and about their promises to take a Bible course.

Laughter and ridicule followed. Many had their lessons torn up and flushed down the drain. On the night before the first class graduation, thirty-three weeks later, one member of the faithful few forgot to turn the other cheek while setting some of the men straight on a few things. He showed up for his diploma next day with a black eye. He said he ran into a door.

There was no word or indication on the diploma that it was received in the U. S. Penitentiary. I was not trying to be deceitful, but I was trying to be practical in behalf of the men who were making an honest effort to restore their lives in society. I signed the diploma as director. On the left was the seal of "Community Church, Atlanta, Georgia."

Things didn't always run smoothly. Once, shortly before the final examination, I announced that the exam papers were missing.

"There must be a crook in the house," shouted several of the men.

The men didn't become great Bible expositors, but the study course did something for them. I watched night after night as the inmates sat in their cells grasping at a straw—the Word of God. I had seen their pictures in Post Offices around the nation, with a word underneath—WANTED. And they didn't look quite the same sitting in prison reading the Bible.

More and more men began to take the course when they saw its effects on others. In six years a total of 1,850 graduated.

Other prisons around the country began to hear about the course and wrote for information. Requests were received from Texas, California, Pennsylvania, Alabama and many other states. Copies were placed in outstanding Christian universities of America and Europe. Oxford and Cambridge were given copies.

I don't think I can ever forget the inspiring days when murderers, rapists, thieves and drug addicts walked proudly onto the platform before their fellow prisoners and received diplomas.

An insight into the Bible course was found one day in the institution magazine, written by an inmate. The story, entitled, "The Fix," read, in part:

"Whatcha got in the envelope, Joe?"

"My Bible course lessons."

"Your what?"

"Bible course lessons."

"I thought you missed out on parole over six months ago."

"I did."

"Then what's the score? Why are you still fooling around with that thing?"

"I don't know. Guess maybe I got hooked on it. It gets more interestin' every lesson."

"Brother, I've seen everything now. I remember when you started taking that thing. 'Course I thought you were battin' for a parole."

"I was, but I missed it. I don't know what happened, but I didn't seem to want to drop the course for some reason or other."

"What's with the Bible course? It's just about church and stuff, ain't it?"

"It's about the Bible, only it explains it in such a simple way that anyone can understand and realize its value, no matter what his faith is."

"What about a fellow like me that hasn't got no faith in particular? Would it make sense to me?"

"Look, I was never much of a bug for religion. Fact of the matter is, I never even gave the Bible a thought until I started taking this cell-study course. But I'm telling you it's a pretty sound thing. You can figure it out for yourself. I used to be a pretty rank character. Couldn't even get along with myself, let alone with others. I think it sort of helps a guy to find himself."

"Say, you're coming on pretty strong there, ain't you?"

"Yeah, I guess maybe I am, but you asked me, didn't you?"

"Sure I did. And I noticed you are a different guy, too. You think if I took one of these Bible courses the fellows would rib me about it?"

"The guys in my cell are all sour-graping my takin' it, but every time I get a lesson they glance over my shoulder and start arguing about Moses and Saint Paul and everything. One of the guys blows a carton of cigarette butts on a bet about who Cain bumped off. It went on and on until I had to either get them a course to argue about or never get a chance to work on mine. So I tell them to drop up and see Reverend Tucker. One guy does, and he won't let the other guy see it, so the other guy gets hot and gets himself one. Now they are all wrapped up in it even more than I am."

45

"What do you think about that? You know, I heard Pete make some cracks out in the yard the other day—now that I think of it, I bet he's taking one of them things."

"I know he is."

"Aw, go on."

"It's a fact. They're beginning to come out in the open with it. I've seen guys who missed parole two or three years ago luggin' religious books from the library and you ought to go up to church some Sunday. They have almost as big a turnout as the movies."

"Well, I'll be a. . . . You think they'd give me one of them courses if I went up there?"

"Sure they will. I know them clerks. They're a couple of nice guys. I'll put in a good word for you."

The message of hope and salvation was brought to men at the penitentiary by outstanding ministers of the world, but I began to realize more and more that preaching to the prisoners required a specialized training. They wanted it straight, with no holier-than-thou stuff and no beating around the bush.

Several years ago the pastor of a large church coaxed me into letting him speak. I knew he wasn't trained for the institution ministry and it was with a reluctant heart that I agreed.

I introduced him at the Sunday service and then sat down front with one of my "deacons," who came from a notorious background.

The minister began by saying, "Shall we pray?" He bowed his head and we bowed ours. I shuddered when he uttered an old cliché, "Iron bars and walls do not a prison make." He had just finished the last word when the "deacon" nudged me in the ribs and said, "Chaplain, I have been having hallucinations for the last ten years."

The service was ruined beyond repair. The men lost interest before he began.

He preached on the subject of the prodigal son. An inmate remarked, as he left the auditorium, "If I hear another sermon on the prodigal son, I will be able to preach it myself."

Many of my ministerial friends who came to the prison thought the prodigal son was the only message—the selfish, wicked son away from his father's home. Far greater results were obtained with messages of therapy lifting Christ up, with less emphasis on condemnation.

Inmates voted a sermon on "Saints and Sinners" as their favorite one year. It was about the Good Samaritan—an injured man needing help, only to have so-called religious people pass him by.

The sermon came from something that happened shortly after I began institution work. A man brought me a piece of poetry as his latest creation. Being a novice, I accepted it and acclaimed him a prison Longfellow. Years later, I was reading an old prison magazine, 1912 edition. On the last page was the same poem, captioned, "Saints and Sinners." During the years, this piece of poetry has been claimed by many a man in prison, but I doubt if the author ever will be known. The three paragraphs seemed full of wisdom:

When some fellow yields to temptation
And breaks a conventional law,
We look for no good in his make-up
But God how we look for a flaw;
No one will ask, "How tempted?"
Nor allow for the battles he's fought;
His name becomes food for the jackals,
For us who have never been caught!

He has sinned, we shout from the housetops,
We forget the good that he's done;
We center on one lost battle,
And forget the times he has won;
"Come gaze on the sinner," we thunder,
"And by his examples be taught,
That his footsteps lead to destruction,"
Cry we who have never been caught!

I'm a sinner, O Lord, and I know it,
I'm weak, I blunder and fail;
I'm tossed on life's stormy ocean,
Like ships embroiled in a gale.
I'm willing to trust in Thy mercy,
To keep the commandments Thou has taught,
But deliver me, Lord, from the judgment
Of saints who have never been caught!

SEVEN CONVERTS

S EVEN PRISONERS WERE sitting in my office on this particular Saturday morning. They had come for a group therapy session "to see what made them tick."

It wasn't quite time to start the discussion, and a little good-natured banter was going on among them. Occasionally, I tossed in a word.

The men, judging by appearances, could have been members of a business discussion group, if their clothing had been cut somewhat sharper. They knew their way around in a conversation.

A broom was being wielded around the room by Joe, an aging Negro better known as "Dynamite," who grinned most all the time. "Dynamite" had been quite a man in his prime. He had fought Jack Johnson, the heavyweight champ, and a lot of the other big boys. But the money finally ran out and he broke the law to get some more. He was caught.

I looked around the room at this strange collection of men, from such varied backgrounds. And my thoughts wandered in recalling incidents from the lives of each.

There was Willie, a nice-looking fellow who had once made $100,000 a year stealing cars. One night, after I had spoken at an Elks convention concerning my prison work, an FBI agent came up to me and asked, somewhat humorously: "Tell me, chaplain, do you rehabilitate *all* the criminals we send you?"

I decided I could best answer that question by asking one myself: "Tell me, Mr. FBI agent, do you catch *all* the crooks?"

Then I asked him if he knew a fellow named Willie S——. "Do I?" he fairly shouted. "We spent thousands of dollars chasing and convicting that character. He was on our most-wanted list for two years. We finally got him salted away for five years. Do you know where he is now?"

"Yes," I replied, looking at my watch, "at this moment he should be in Cell 4-32, 'B' Cell House, Atlanta Penitentiary, grading examination papers in a Bible course he is helping me teach to inmates."

The FBI man looked a little shocked.

I continued:

"You fellows spent a lot of money to sew him up for five years. I spent only a three-cent postage stamp and I have him sewed up for eternity."

We discussed Willie's bizarre story for a while before I told him about the stamp.

Life was too tame for him in the little town on the West Coast. He liked people, and lots of them. In a nearby city he found a job as an automobile salesman. Soon, with his quick mind and glib tongue, he was making $125 a week. And this was back when $50 a week put a man in the executive class. He married, bought a profitable auto business, joined various civic clubs, a church, and mixed socially with the best people in town.

Like so many other get-rich-quicks, Willie began to live beyond his ample means. This and gambling put him $25,000 in the red. Having borrowed to the limit on his personal credit, he began to "double finance" cars and to obtain bank loans on various forms of hypothecated securities. Getting in deeper all the time, with loans coming due at a rapid rate, he decided on a drastic measure of forging checks and dealing in stolen cars. He had one "trusted employee" on the lot.

The police "bunco" squad became suspicious when it developed that more than a dozen wealthy men, whose bank accounts had been tapped for substantial sums by forged checks, had at some time done business with Willie's firm. This seemed to be more than coincidence. They showed photographs of Willie to bank tellers who had cashed the checks. One teller positively identified him as the man who used a fictitious name in cashing a $2,000 check.

Officers thought they had an airtight case. But after a week-long trial, at which Willie paraded a dozen character witnesses to the stand and was represented by the best legal counsel money could buy, the jury acquitted him. He threw a celebration house party that cost over $1,500 and was attended by dozens of respectable friends—including the pastor of his church. (He was a liberal contributor.)

A few months later he was indicted for complicity in a bank robbery. Many FBI agents worked nearly a year building their case against him. There was a massive array of evidence—his fingerprints on "hot money," partial identification by several witnesses, papers from the getaway car found in an office he had rented under an assumed name, tags from the getaway car found in his personal car, which he was driving when arrested.

But again Willie had enough money, borrowed or stolen, for a first-rate defense. The FBI lost another case.

Soon afterwards, however, the "trusted employee" was induced to "sing." In rapid succession, Willie was tried and convicted of such crimes as perjury, grand larceny and interstate transportation of stolen cars. Sentences totaled thirteen years. In 1947 he entered a Federal prison to serve the years. Most men would have given up, but Willie didn't. His money gone, he decided to study law and appeal his own cases. He was almost a genius at his new role, and was well grounded with the practical experience he had received at his trials. He was successful in obtaining reversals, on legal technicalities, of all the convictions. In 1950 he walked out a free man.

There was no happy reunion with his wife. She said she was tired of living with the fear of a "knock on the door." With eight dollars in his pocket, Willie dropped from sight. He was next heard from in 1951, when his picture appeared in Post Offices over the caption: "WANTED BY THE FBI."

For two years the agents looked for him. He was a one-man crime wave. He forged checks and stole expensive cars. Along the way, he picked up a night club hostess as a traveling companion. Managing to stay about two jumps ahead of the agents, they lived in Miami, Havana or Mexico City in the winter, and moved north to expensive lake resorts in the summer. Fantastic sums of money were spent.

Willie's paramour liked the excitement. She thought it was delightfully clever the way they eluded the FBI. One day as they were driving along, she said: "We should write a book on 'How We Fooled the FBI.'" Willie, not a man to underrate the opposition, replied: "I think we had better wait a while. Let's not be premature."

His caution proved to be well advised. That same night he was recognized by a hotel clerk. Newspapers next day carried accounts of the arrest of "one of the most wanted car thieves in the nation."

A legal battle, lasting two years, followed. He finally

made a deal to plead guilty to two counts, with the understanding all other Federal charges would be dropped and he would receive a total sentence of five years.

This was the point at which I interviewed Willie in the Admission-Orientation Unit of the Atlanta Penitentiary. He was polite and answered questions courteously, but I had the feeling he was absolutely indifferent to religion. He was assigned to a clerical job and I saw little of him for several months.

One day I saw him talking to one of my clerks in the office lobby. He was inquiring about a birthday card for his mother. I invited him in for a chat and picked out an especially attractive card for him.

I have a theory that every criminal is a soul in the sight of God, and no matter how depraved, has a soft spot somewhere in his heart—a "button" that can be pushed to turn him on and off. I was sure I had found Willie's "button"—his mother, a devout Christian woman.

"How would you like me to write your mother and tell her how you're getting along?" I asked. I knew he had a good institutional record, had donated blood to a local charity hospital, was active in inmate welfare activities and had received a special reward of "Meritorious Good Time."

His face lit up and tears came to his eyes. "Chaplain Tucker," he said with deep emotion, "there is nothing in the world I would appreciate more than such a letter."

That was the way in which I invested three cents of the government's money and won a soul for Christ. Willie began attending church, Sunday school and Bible Forums. He volunteered to help in the office during his spare time. He joined my group therapy session. He read his Bible and borrowed religious books. Soon he was helping me grade exam papers. When a group of more than a hundred ministers visited the institution, Willie helped conduct the service, an all-inmate production.

(Willie is now a free man, and a changed one. We taught him how the love of God could return him to the place in society he had once known.)

The bull session in my office was still going strong. I glanced over at Jones, a man who had a way with words. He had won oratorical contests as a youth. It seemed rather natural that he should attend a Bible College and be a minister. He completed the three-year course in two years and graduated with honors. On the side, thanks to his typing and shorthand, he earned extra money doing secretarial work for the administrators.

Jones married and for several years was considered one of the brightest young men in his church denomination. Everything was going his way until he became involved with another woman and surrendered his license. His wife remained faithful and was a good mother to their children.

He got into the real estate business and found the biggest money in unethical practices. Then came forged checks and stolen automobiles and arrest. I conducted a routine admission interview with him a few days after his arrival. I expressed special sympathy for his situation because of his ministerial background and remarked:

"You made a poor trade in exchanging the Lord for women and crime."

He told me later that he was never able to shake off the comment, although he seldom attended prison services. It was a year or so later that I was able to do him a favor. He wasn't receiving any letters from his wife and couldn't understand why. I discovered a clerical error had been made in the mail office. The letters from his wife and mother were being returned with the notation that he had been paroled. Within thirty minutes of his complaint, he was talking with his wife on the telephone call I had arranged. He wasn't able to blink back the tears as he talked with his wife and boys.

After that he attended church and Sunday school regularly, but there was a stumbling block that prevented his complete surrender to God. He was obsessed with the idea that no one could have confidence in him because he had been a minister before taking up crime. We had many private talks and he became a leader in the psychotherapy sessions. Finally he reached the place of believing in the forgiveness of God through Christ in spite of his grave disobedience.

Jones became the teacher of the Bible Forum, in which fifty inmates participated regularly. He won the respect and admiration of other inmates with his sincerity and Christian spirit of helpfulness.

(During the last several months of his term, Jones took vocational training in brick masonry. His offenses had made it difficult for him to follow a professional type of work, and he turned to a more menial skill to earn his living. His literary talents became a hobby and relaxation from the physical work.)

Jack was leading the office conversation when I glanced at him. The inmates had coined a description for Jack after hearing his story. They said he "had a wheel in his head that just went backwards."

A fine-looking young man and athletically inclined, he could have had a college scholarship from high school, but decided to get married instead. He worked at a gas station and then moved upward as salesman for a national concern.

Jack and his wife talked over the limitations they faced as high-school graduates and decided on college in spite of the evident hardships. They moved to a college town and began their courses. On the side, Jack worked as assistant football coach and his wife found odd jobs in town. They kept up the religious activities they had known since childhood.

Money was scarce, but their enterprising spirit could not be whipped. They graduated together, returned home and accepted teaching jobs. There still wasn't enough money—a condemnation of the teaching pay scale. Jack might have escaped prison if politicians had thought enough of America's children to pay the teachers as much as that made by street sweepers.

One day, after all his years of hard work and sacrifice, Jack pulled a bandana over his face and walked into a bank. With a gun pointed at the teller, he said: "This is a stickup." He had a car waiting and took off fast with the money. Within an hour he was captured and placed in jail.

The inmates were right. "He had a wheel in his head that just went backward."

One of the most heart-rending things I have seen in my life as a prison chaplain came the day his aged mother, beautiful wife and toddling children came down the long hall for a visit.

(During his stay in prison Jack re-dedicated his life to Christ. He played on the baseball team, helped in showing the movies, sang in the choir and was a model inmate. He has been reunited with his family and regards the prison sentence as a long, black dream.)

My eyes wandered over to Guy. He was the juvenile delinquent, a term some officers have described as sugarcoated words for criminals. He came from a broken home.

Guy began by stealing candy, cokes and bicycles. He spent a lot of time in pool halls. He had a gang. The rackets and reformatory followed. He took a postgraduate course in crime at the institution, and was one of the leaders during a mutiny over the food situation.

Along with several bad actors, he was sent to Atlanta, with added sentences. I tried to help Guy and the other kids, but I must confess they were dynamite incarnate. Guy smoked about seven cigars a day. They were tilted at a forty-five degree angle.

Finally he began to take stock, saw he was getting nowhere fast. He asked his cell officer for help and was referred to me.

He could be titled the "miracle of 1954" because of God's grace. He is remarried, has a daughter and is working hard at a job.

(Guy wrote something for the prison magazine before his release. He said, "At the age of twenty-four, I must shamefully confess to having spent many of them in prison. I wanted to be tough. I hated the thought that anyone could do anything better than I could. If you broke one law, I would break two. But there was something inside crying for me to give God a chance. I had never given Him a chance. I thought about all the razzing I would have to take. Jesus Christ was nailed to a cross for all sinners who wished to be saved . . . and I stood there shrinking at being talked about. One night, in bed, I called to Jesus, 'Lord, I would like to give You my life. Forgive my sins, they are many. Make a decent man of me.' Thank God, He has done just that.")

Bill ambled over to the office water cooler. He was a five-time loser and often bragged that his family back in the hills had made moonshine liquor for generations. In fact, they fought a war with Uncle Sam over it, "The Whiskey Rebellion."

Each member in the family had done time, with the exception of his mother, and she had been on probation twice. They believed it was their constitutional right to make "corn," and pointed out that it was easier to carry downhill in a bottle instead of a wagon. The two places Bill called home were the Ozarks and Atlanta.

Once he went to New York to do some bootlegging on a larger scale. The installation in the heart of the city was one of great secrecy and the mechanical make-up was fabulous. Burlap was creosoted to kill the smell of fumes. Things went great for months and money was rolling in, but when he reported for work one day a hand reached out. It was attached to a Federal Revenue agent.

One of Bill's buddies at the institution asked him to attend religious services.

"If I couldn't get religion on the streets, I'm not going to get it in jail," he replied.

The buddy insisted and Bill came along for the walk. God spoke to his heart. He said later that God had been explained in a language he could understand.

(Bill returned to the Ozarks and built a church with his own hands. When it was completed the people asked him to be the pastor. He accepted, but didn't confine his religion to the church. Each time the Federal Court convened, he addressed the men about to leave for prison. He told them about his wasted years before finding new life in Christ.)

A man we knew as Ose was the only Negro in the psychotherapy group. He was guilty of his crime, as were most all the others, but his case was unusual.

He worked his way up to chief petty officer in the Navy before World War II, when ratings were hard to get. Superiors cited him a number of times for outstanding service.

His ship was anchored at Pearl Harbor on Dec. 7, 1941, when the Jap planes came over. Escape was measured in inches, as other vessels went up in smoke all around. The ship became a part of the little fleet that will go down in history for its gallant and bulldoggish attitude toward the big Japanese fleet during the lean days of United States recovery.

Twice during the next year the ship was hit. Casualties were many. The crew was ordered to the States for a rest. During the period on the coast, Ose took a service revolver and robbed a bank. He said he wanted to help his buddies who were killed.

Ose was sentenced to ten years at Atlanta. He was awfully mixed up when he came, but settled down after a while and accepted the term in good spirits. From this beginning, he made the time serve him instead of his serving time.

He never cursed a judge and had no bitter words for attorneys or officers.

Within a year Ose was one of the outstanding electricians in the institution. He attended church, sang in the choir and was the one thousandth student to graduate from the Bible course.

(Now in sunny California, Ose has been reunited with his wife and family. I have received reports that he is still singing in the choir and is teaching in the Sunday school. His job—electrician in a large department store just out of Los Angeles.)

Whitey, the last member of our group, was an alcoholic. He managed to get to the ninth grade in school before being expelled.

After marrying his school sweetheart, he got a job as weaver in a cotton mill and did pretty well until he took his first sociable drink. Within a matter of months, he had to have whiskey and would do anything to get it.

Whitey told me he once rode a motorcycle from New York to Boston and back without realizing he had taken a ride. Drunkenness, vagrancy, and family abuse charges came often. A well-meaning but ill-advised family would get him off the hook.

He stole a car and took off for the southwest, where he sold Bibles and sharecropped to get enough whiskey. Officers caught up and brought him to Atlanta.

With his mill background, Whitey became a model hand in the weave room. He came to the services and made his peace with God.

(He was a shining example of the rehabilitation program when he left, and I guess I did a lot of bragging. Within six months he was back. It was a fresh reminder that I was dealing with humans, with human weaknesses. I started all over again. Whitey received his old job and his place in the choir. It seemed he had never left.

He has now completed the second term and is at his home in Maine, doing well.)

As I continued to look around the room at the seven converts, I marveled again at the message God had used to change hardened criminals into cheerful Christians.

The same message of Christ had been lived before them and preached to all, with their varied backgrounds. In every sermon I had tried to show the men what God could do in any life, no matter what the circumstances.

For an illustration of flesh and blood they could see, I used myself. I told them how God had reached deep into the bowels of the earth to spare the life of a dying coal miner and how He had led me each step of the way to my position as chaplain at the prison.

It seemed to help. They looked at the false hand hanging from my sleeve and knew I was giving it to them straight. A simple testimony seemed to be the key that unlocked the hearts of the seven converts.

In much the same manner that I have told the prisoners about my life, I would like to tell it to you.

SCHOOL DAZE AND
MINE TALK

I WOULD HAVE BEEN born in Pittston, Pennsylvania, if the coal miners hadn't been on strike. My father went down the Susquehanna River to nearby Sunbury and found temporary work. The event occurred there.

A football team of boys entered the world on our street that night—October 1, 1909. All were born with assistance from a Pennsylvania Dutch midwife. She charged my parents ten dollars and I have the receipt.

Soon afterwards, the strike was settled and the family returned to Pittston.

My school career was erratic, almost from the first day

FREE RELIGIOUS LITERATURE, SUPPLIED BY THE CHURCHES, IS
DISTRIBUTED FROM A RACK IN THE CHAPLAIN'S OFFICE.

INMATE LEADERS AND THE CHAPLAIN PLAN EASTER SERVICES.

of enrollment, when mother dressed me in my Sunday clothes—short pants, Buster Brown coat, tie and straw hat. She tried to encourage me by saying I might become President of the United States if I studied hard.

Mother, a great saint of God whose family came to America from Scotland, bordered on the edge of a white lie in suggesting the Presidency for her balky offspring. Traditionally, our family had been Republicans and there hadn't been a Republican President for twenty-five years.

It may be that I instituted the Reciprocal Trade Act into the elementary schools of Pennsylvania. In routine order, I advanced through the first, second and third grades, then back to the second, up to the fourth, back to third and on to sixth and seventh. Studies were far from easy, mainly because such things as spring breezes and then snow-covered hills kept my spirit far away from books.

When the bell rang, I usually was first out the door, not a mean feat, considering the competition from a lot of other restless fellows. I raced down the stairs one day and went speeding for the door before seeing that it was filled by a visiting professor. It was too late to stop and I smacked him in the stomach like a Notre Dame fullback. The impact knocked the wind out of him and left me sprawled on the floor. This was my first formal introduction to the professor of the Pittston educational system. He was a good sport, however, and no disciplinary action was taken.

One of my greatest joys was getting out of school to

attend funerals. All the relatives would come from miles around. While the women busied themselves in the kitchen, the men folk blanketed the yard with cigarette smoke. Most of the other children romped in the yard, but I always chose to sit on father's knee and listen to stories told by the miners. They related, in great detail, about the Twin Mine explosion and the fifty-six men lost in a grave hundreds of feet below the surface—how the whole area mourned as the children and widows screamed . . . about the old West Pittston shaft disaster when a piece of equipment caught fire and men were asphyxiated in the underground chambers. When rescuers found the dead men, the bodies were clinging together, some in an attitude of prayer and some with terrified looks.

The stories would go on and on until the funeral service began. Then would come the procession to the cemetery, where the mine disaster stories were verified by countless monuments. Words seemed to ring in my heart—"don't be a miner"—"don't be a miner." But father, who had come from England, and practically all of my other relatives, were "men of the pit" in America and the homeland. I had great respect for them. Somehow, the fears seemed to fade in the light of exciting, dangerous opportunities.

School was something else. It wasn't even practical. The philosophy of the average miner was that work constituted the important thing, along with having a home.

I was a husky, elongated, rebellious youth of fourteen, with the whole social world seemingly against me, when I "graduated" from the seventh grade with "honors" for indifference. This was a red-letter day. The teacher had a twisted smile on her face and edge of temper in her voice when she said, "There are two smart people in this room. I'm one of them. Park Tucker, you're the other. Will you please leave the room—and the school. In fact, it would be better to stay home than waste your time in this place."

Never had I known such unbounded joy. This was my graduation day. School was over. I had all the knowledge I would need in life. With a big grin, I walked out.

Things seemed even better when I reached the deserted schoolyard and heard the familiar, hated sounds coming from the various rooms. Taking a last look back at the halls of learning, I shouted:

"Fare thee well, Alma Mater! I never did like thee."

Down the street of the mining town I went, out of a world of wistful dreaming into one of vibrant reality. But I wasn't quite ready to meet the big, familiar, grime-blackened man in overalls and helmet when he spotted me on the street.

"H-h-hello, dad," I stammered.

"Son, you're home early from school," he said, showing a stern, old-country look that pierced my soul.

"Guess what happened today in school?" I said.

"Same thing that happened before?" he countered.

"Yes, dad."

"Come in the house and let's talk about it."

With lagging feet, I dragged into the kitchen for a lecture on life from a postgraduate in the University of Hard Knocks.

"Well, son," he began, "tomorrow you'll start in one of the greatest schools in the world, where a man makes his way, and earns his bread and butter with the sweat of his brow."

His words sounded like poetry. But it was a little different next morning. At five o'clock, long before the sun came up, father's deep voice boomed: "Come on, son; it's time for work." There was a power in his voice that I heeded rapidly.

I pulled on the new uniform of a miner and all the extra equipment that went with it. Mother, showing lines of worry, watched from the door as I started out with father.

Down the tracks we walked with the other men. The day before I had been a young kid on the school lot— fighting, running, yelling with the other boys. Now I was a man of the world—a miner. The hardened men who walked beside us to the pit were Irish, Scotch, Italian, Polish, men who had come to America from all over the world to work deep in the earth.

Many already had gathered as we approached the pit entrance. "Throw out your chest, son, and look like a man," father said. I tried, but it was hard, with my overalls turned up five times and size twenty-one jacket altered to fit a fourteen-year-old.

Then came a big moment, the first talk with my boss.

"Well, Joe, is this the boy?"

"Yes, John."

The foreman's steady look didn't miss a thing.

"All right, start him in," he said.

My short interview was over. I was qualified to enter the workings of the underworld.

The hum of machinery and noises of men busying themselves for the day's task were fascinating, a real education. There was the powder car, loaded with enough explosives to move the pit a couple of miles if detonated. I looked over the supplies of drills and picks used in the extraction of "black diamonds."

The cage whistle sounded, a signal that the elevator was ready to take miners to the various levels. Ten men formed a load. I watched as the cage dropped out of sight into the unknown, with only a quivering steel rope to tell whether it was under control of the hoisting engineer.

My time came and I entered the cage with father. It was an exciting moment. All the old hands were smiling at "Joe's boy," the greenhorn.

The slight sway of the cage brought to mind again all the stories I had heard as a boy about mine disasters. I remembered the man who had lived next door. He was an engineer. He and his assistants were testing the mine elevator one day when the floor gave way. They fell sixteen hundred feet to the bottom. I remembered the funeral and the cemetery.

I snapped back to attention when someone in the cage said, "It's three hundred feet below." Cold sweat formed on my brow. The earth seemed to drop out from under. Dim lamps on the caps lighted the speedily passing shaft cribbing. The dripping cold water felt like a stabbing knife. By the time I became adjusted to the speed, the engineer began applying the brakes. The effect on my stomach was beyond description. It seemed that I had to reach up for my dinner pail.

This was a new world. The underground city was like the ones I had read and dreamed about. Whitewashed sides of the mine stood out. The foreman had an office at the bottom, and there was a first-aid compartment, where many men had departed from the living.

Big rats ran out from hidden dens to tug at pieces of food offered by some of the men. This was a way for the men to kill time as they got ready for long walks to far reaches of the mine.

A coal train came into sight. Noise increased as the train traveled along the narrow-gauge track. These were the cars allocated to miners for loading.

I was given a copper metal check, number 602. And I was assigned a mule, the real workhorse, so to speak, of mining. Her name was Nellie. She was a star in the eating department, but the old gal was smart, too. In spots where only an experienced miner could find his way out, Nellie needed only the welcome command, "Home, girl." Off she would trot, up and down heading roads, through rock tunnels, up plains and straight to her stall in the barn.

Nellie was blind. She had spent most of her life in the dark earth.

Many times I tried to figure out what kept her in the middle of the road, never missing a step to the right or left. Years later I asked a university professor about it. Nellie was a mystery to the Ph.D., too. God must have given her something humans didn't possess—a special intuition that overcame darkness, elevations and depressions.

The day came when I had to say goodbye to Nellie. We were taking cars filled with coal down a steep grade when the brakes failed. The cars picked up momentum and poor Nellie could not keep pace. Her death warrant came when she stumbled and fell. A sickening, crushing sound followed. I didn't want to look, but trimmed my light and watched as Nellie looked up. She was suffering badly. A miner buried his pick in her head.

(One of my greatest joys in life came later when I heard that mules had been replaced in mines by electric motors.)

More responsible positions came gradually, and finally the day arrived when I could apply for the designation of full-fledged miner—like my father, grandfather and ancestors in Scotland. My horizon may have been infinitely small, but my pulse raced the day I received the mining "papers." Other papers and sheepskins of much greater value were to come afterwards, but none compared with the mining recognition.

One of the reasons for such unrivaled importance was my admiration for a tall, well-built miner named George. Most of the men looked up to him. I was no exception. I tried to model my life on his example. He carried a "bud dust" sack for smokes in the upper part of his overalls. I did the same. I gathered enough courage once to talk rough to the others like George did. Once was enough. The bruises inflicted on my face convinced me that I needed a few more years and a little added muscle for rough talk.

MAKING OF A MAN

Saloons lined both sides of the main street in our town. They were crowded most of the time with miners. Not wanting to miss a thing, I went along for the joy ride.

The religious ways of my parents were strange and unwelcome. A godly life didn't compare with a night on the town with the boys. I was the prodigal son . . . but I was living at home.

Mother came from a fine, middle-class, God-fearing family in Scotland. Father was a product of the YMCA's early efforts in the mining district. One Sunday afternoon, as a young man of twenty-three, he was on the way to meet the boys at their favorite saloon when a

"Y" worker asked him to attend the service. He went, for some reason, and was converted. Old things passed away. I have wondered often what my lot might have been if the unkown "Y" worker hadn't stopped my father and offered him a new life in Jesus Christ. I had seen the homes of drunken miners. They were a new low in life. I insisted I could quit drinking before reaching that state.

Night after night, mother asked me the same question, "Son, why don't you become a Christian?" I brushed the question aside as often as it was asked. Father was a man of few words, but he didn't have to speak. He troubled me when he sat at his place in the kitchen and, with folded hands, prayed for me.

My heart cried out, "What's wrong with me?" And the inner voice answered, "You're all right; you're all right." Off I would go again for my nightly fling.

During those difficult days, father's health broke. One day, it seemed, he was the picture of health, a real miner in the pit, and the next he was a feeble old man. The wheezing breath marked his disease as "miner's asthma," an illness well known in our town.

From this point on, I was the main support of the family. I was a veteran of seven years in the mines. No longer was I a greenhorn. My body was tough. It had to be for the job of shoveling twenty to forty tons of coal a day.

I was what miners call a "mucker," and often worked in places no more than four feet high. Mother bought me two pads used by wash women. I tied them on my knees with wire and walked on my knees for as long as eight hours.

The men didn't go outside for fresh air until the day's work was done. We ate in the mine. I talked to my brother-in-law in the section once and he didn't know who I was. My face and teeth were black.

The work was hard, but there was always Saturday night to bolster my morale. Saturday night in a mining town has never been adequately described. I appreciated the usual wine, women and song more than people in other professions, because of the joy of having them on top of the ground.

Saturday, October 22, 1932, dawned like most of the others. I met the day when it was young, at five o'clock. The sun was coming over the mountains and the valley awaited the welcoming warmth of another day.

I made my way to the pit. Bill, Roy, Mike and the others in my section were standing around.

It seemed like any other day, except the men were a little happier because it was Saturday. A man at the cage yelled, "Ten more men." We jumped on. I had no way of knowing as we stood there in the swaying cage that God was evaluating ten coal miners on the scales of life. Down, down, down, we went into the earth.

I picked up my part of the supplies and started off on the half-hour hike to the far end of the mine. The job that day was robbing pillars, a dangerous game of "stealing" the remainder of the standing coal and then allowing the chamber to cave in.

After lunch, while the tools were being readied, we

waited for the cars. A brakeman yelled, "Tucker, how many cars?"

I shouted back, "Seven, drop in six and put one on the branch."

When the six cars were placed in the chamber, we started work on the large pile of coal blasted the day before by six-foot dynamite holes. Roy and I worked steadily, within a few feet of each other. Large pieces of coal were shoved along the sides of the cars. Miners call this "topping," for added weight. On each finished car I marked my number, 602, with chalk. The marking was important. Cars taken out on the cage were placed on the weightmaster's scales. He would sing out, "Tucker, miner 602, fifty-seven hundredweight." This was recorded. On the fifteenth and thirtieth of each month, the figures were totaled and we received our pay accordingly. The miner's first interest each day on returning to the surface was to check the weightmaster's returns. Descriptive adjectives used by disgruntled men kept the master's hair curled.

When the six cars had been hauled away, we could hear the rumbling of another—the seventh and final. It would be a breeze.

I noticed rats as they ran from the workings, a traditional danger sign to the miner, and speculated on how long it would take to get clear of danger. It was a mere run of thirty minutes and then a cage trip of sixteen hundred feet to the surface. But I dismissed such thoughts from my mind. This was Saturday, one-thirty in the afternoon, only one car to load, and the big night ahead.

Roy was shoveling alongside the car and I was in the blind end. While setting up the topping, I turned and saw a large piece of coal. I lifted it and was regaining my stance when I heard a rumbling noise. This one didn't sound like cars coming. It sounded like a hurricane. The mine began to tremble. Pieces of coal scattered from the sides. There was a terrible crushing noise and a giant hit me from behind. I found myself half buried in dirt, slime and rock, numb all over—in total darkness.

"The world has come to an end," I thought. "It's one of the stories I heard as a boy . . . coming true. It's a story—only this time I'm an actor in it."

Then my mind faced reality and warned, "Run for your life; it's an explosion." But I couldn't run. By moving with desperation, I managed to stand, and catch hold of the beam in the seventh car.

Rock continued to fall. A huge piece of soapstone dropped from the roof and mangled my left arm. I thought about Nellie when she was crushed. I had a passionate desire to live and tried to climb over the car with my mutilated hand. Sides of the mine suddenly caved in with a roar and the floor buckled. The seventh car, with its human wreck on top, turned over. I was buried alive—under a steel car and sixteen hundred feet of rock.

The ear-splitting noises of the explosion were followed

by an unreal quietness. Then I heard the pathetic cries of dying men. Stories of yesterday came to mind about uncles and other relatives who had died like this. I pictured people gathering on the surface, an ambulance rushing through town, emergency preparations being made at the hospital, my mother hearing the news, wicker baskets from the undertakers.

I heard a voice, very weak, calling my name—"Park . . . Park." It flashed through my mind that I had heard the voice because I was dying. But again it came from the darkness . . . "Park."

With my uninjured hand, I managed to ignite my lamp with one strike. In the dirty, smoky air, I looked for the owner of the voice. The car covered my body, but I could move my head.

I saw Roy, and was horrified. He was held in a vise, the car crushing him on one side and rocks on the other. With a broken back and crudely-amputated legs, he cried, helplessly:

"Park, Park, pray for me."

I didn't know how to pray. But Roy was dying. I had to try!

As the blood was squeezed from him, I cried:

"Oh, God, help Roy. Oh, God, help Bill . . . and Lord, help me. Be merciful to us sinners . . . in Jesus' name."

In that awful condition, I saw Roy for the last time as the pieces of rock slowly covered us. In my grave, slowly being filled by nature, a battle of life and death took place. I didn't want to die. I was too young, only twenty-three. I could see the roof coming closer and closer. I touched it with my hand.

The creeping rocks caused my legs to break. It was a weird sound to hear my own bones breaking. I counted ten breaks, but there were more.

Years before I had seen other men in similar conditions. I watched a young Polish boy as he lay in the dark coal dirt and heard him mumble, "Broshna, Broshna." This was his call for God. The next time it was a poor victim crying out, "Mother of Christ." I was puzzled during these times about the strange thing that made rough miners, who never thought about God, call out to Him when near death.

Now I was doing the same. My blackened face was being washed by tears and my heart began to break. A big, ungodly miner, I cried out like a six-year-old child, "Oh, Lord, have mercy on me." I gave up my life to God. And I promised that if I did come out alive I would serve Him for the rest of my days, in any way that He wanted to use me.

God heard my voice! He came and stood beside the seventh car . . . with all of His love, mercy and kindness. He "brought me up from the horrible pit, out of the miry clay, and set my feet upon a rock."

I knew that a rescue crew was doing more than its best to reach the underground tomb before air and life ran out for all the trapped men.

Working frantically, the rescuers burrowed through awesome piles of debris, broken rails and smashed cars.

The break-through finally came, but no one had enough strength left to cheer. One man was already dead and others were dying.

Bodies were taken out as fast as they could be uncovered.

God had rescued the most important part of me, my soul, a few minutes before. Now my mangled body was to be given a chance. I was administered emergency first aid, placed on a stretcher and taken to the foot of the shaft for the trip to the top.

As they placed a blanket over me, I heard a miner say:

"Well, that's Tucker's last trip up."

When I was placed on the floor of the cage, the footman telephoned to the engineer, "John, take it easy this trip. We have miner 602 on."

Gently, I moved toward the surface. The small light, far above, seemed to represent the light of Christ coming into my heart—first, small and far away, then larger and larger. As the cage neared the surface, God said: "Park if you will be in Christ, you will be a new creature; old things will pass away and all things will become new."

Then daylight flooded my heart and eyes!

A buddy, who had planned to go dancing with me that evening, was leaving the hospital after visiting his sister. He stopped to watch as the ambulances unloaded their pieces of humanity. The first victim he spotted was his happy-go-lucky friend, Tucker. It made a great impression on him. He told me later he never attended the dance.

Emergency operations came quickly, and I was taken to the ward. Delirious and in a state of shock, I was not sure whether I was dead or alive. In the blur I could still hear Bill crying out for help, Roy asking me to pray, and my own soul pleading for the Lord. My condition grew steadily worse. Gangrene poisoning was working in my arm. My weight dropped to 120 pounds.

The red lines of poisoning could be seen more clearly each day as they went up my arm and moved toward the shoulder. Surgeons used all their skills, but had to amputate in spite of my weakened condition.

Day after day I was on the brink of death. The crisis came on a Sunday evening. Three doctors held a bedside consultation over miner 602—with an amputated arm, legs broken in thirteen places, fractured skull, broken pelvis bones. As they walked away, one said, "He'll be dead in the morning."

But morning never came!

Two great Christians, my mother and father, were at the foot of the bed. On their knees, with tears in their eyes, they prayed: "Oh, God have mercy on our son. If it be Thy will, raise up Park from this bed. . . ."

Doctors were amazed when I rallied.

Life returned gradually. Thirteen months later, two orderlies lifted me out of bed for the first time since the accident. Pitifully weak and thin, with a pinned-up sleeve, I wobbled on scarred legs condemned as useless by the doctors. I took a long look at myself, in comparison to others, before falling back onto the bed in despair. Big tears spilled out as I cried, "Oh, God, what will ever become of me?"

He answered softly, "Son, don't forget that I saved your life. You keep up your end of the covenant, and I'll keep up mine."

Within a few days I was taken home to recuperate.

Mother made a "hospital room at home" for me in the front part of the house so I could look out and watch people as they walked up and down the street.

Before long, I knew most of the going and coming habits of about everybody in Pittston.

The favorite time of my convalescence was the Christmas season, with all of its gaiety and good will toward man. Friends from the Salvation Army and other groups stood outside my window and sang the beautiful carols. It seemed that everyone in Pittston made a special effort to be nice, because they knew I was one of the few survivors of the mine explosion.

An unusual thing occurred between Christmas and New Years, as I continued to watch from the window. In a twentieth-century application to my life, it paralleled the death of Stephen, as recorded in the Bible. Paul stood at the outer gate and watched him stoned to death. I sat in my room as another saint of God died on a nearby doorstep.

The young man who died was named Bob Kohler. He had made a stand for Christ in the high school before going off to college to prepare for the ministry. The

Pittston newspaper announced he was home on a visit and would deliver his first sermon on Sunday night at the First Baptist Church. Many turned out to hear the home-town boy.

Young Bob stood proudly in the pulpit. He chose as his text, "The Wonderful Jesus." After the service, he visited the pastor and his young daughter for a while, leaving at eleven o'clock. He walked down the street and over by our house. As he went around the corner, he fell on the front steps at the house of my late sister, Mrs. John Malone. He had suffered a fatal heart attack. Two days later, he was buried.

Some people regarded it as a tragic end for a young man who had given his life to God. I can't agree. God demanded only one sermon from Bob. A thousand may be demanded of others.

I had promised God I would serve Him, but first I had to learn how to walk again. My mother and the doctor taught me. The braces were taken off and I found I could hobble around the house with crutches. This was extremely difficult, because I had no left arm to grasp the crutch.

Day after day, month after month, cared for by the loving hands of my mother under the sure direction of God, I slowly regained my health.

And the day came when I stood on a solid foundation, ready to take my first big step for God.

THE CHILDREN AND
MR. TUCKER

THE REVEREND HENRY COREY was my pastor, but appearances at his church had been as few and far between as I could make them. On a visit to the house after I had recovered, he said:

"Brother Tucker, your father has told me that you want to be a preacher."

"Yes," I replied, "but I can't be a preacher."

"Was your throat injured in the accident?" he asked.

"No, Reverend," I answered, "I lost ninety-five per cent of my vocabulary when I became a Christian because so much of it was cursing. The last five per cent is made up of words like dese, dose, dem and ain't."

The Reverend Corey seemed stuck. He walked around and scratched his head. Finally he turned and said, "Brother Park, you're illiterate."

Not knowing what the word meant, I thought he was paying me a compliment.

"Praise the Lord," I said, "that should help make me a preacher."

Brother Corey took his hat and went out the door. He was a little baffled.

When he came back I told him I was willing to return to school and asked: "Where do I start? College?"

"You'll start in the seventh grade, where you left off," he said.

"Don't you realize," I stammered, "that the seventh grade is for children and that I'm twenty-five years of age?"

"Children or not, you're headed for the seventh grade," he countered.

This was my first piece of humble pie, but plenty more was to come.

Before returning to school, I went to Wilkes-Barre on a mission I had never expected to make—for the purchase of a left arm and hand. Many strange appliances were tried before I was outfitted with an arm and hand made out of aluminum, iron, brass and canvas glove. I didn't know whether I would ever get used to this foreign thing that hung from my body. People ought to thank God every day for two good hands. The brilliant world of today has jet planes, super-highways, super-trains and super-cars, but no mechanical apparatus ever invented can compare with an ingenious flesh-and-blood hand made by God.

I thought it would be better if I went to another city for my schooling and decided on Wheaton, Illinois, where there was a good Bible academy and college. Money was to come from accident insurance benefits.

Mother, father and the Reverend Corey came down to the railway station to see me off. I had a new suit of clothes and a new suitcase. The farewells were hard, but God helped me as I turned my back on the loved, familiar things in my life. I was still a child at heart at twenty-five.

The train arrived in Wheaton late at night and I found a room in a second-rate hotel. Mother had warned me to "be careful and trust nobody, especially strangers." My body wasn't the only thing under the covers when I went to bed. The suitcase and all my belongings were there, too. Next morning I paid the rent and got out early.

I had never seen a college campus before. My eyes must have looked like half-dollars as I walked across the beautiful grounds, dotted with tall buildings and trees. Girls and boys in casual attire were everywhere. Their clothes didn't look much like mine.

As I approached a building a young gentleman introduced himself and asked, "Are you a new professor here?"

"No," I replied, "I am starting in the seventh grade. Where is it, please?"

"Oh," he said, quite puzzled, "Wheaton Academy is across the street there. Aren't you pretty old to be going to the seventh grade?"

There could be only one reply to that, "Yes, sir."

On the academy grounds a man, by way of making conversation, said, "I presume you're bringing your family to school."

By trying real hard, I was able to keep an edge out of my reply: "No, I am hunting for the seventh grade and I am going to be a minister of the Gospel."

The dean was as amazed as the others when he looked at my two hundred pounds and six feet two inches. But I was duly registered and informed about classes.

That night, I prayed, "Oh, God, please send lots of grace to a big ex-coal miner with one arm and no education."

The grace arrived next morning at eight o'clock, and so did a large group of children. As they walked past my knees, my blood pressure went up a few notches and my face turned crimson.

The teacher joined those who didn't quite know what to make of me. She was a good soul who had taught there for forty years and had never married.

She began by saying, "This is a Christian school. We always begin with a part of Scripture or a prayer, but this morning I have a special Scripture on my heart." She looked right at me and said, "Lo, I have found a man."

I jumped up and said, "Not me. I came here to be a preacher."

The road of intellectualism had started with a bang.

The teacher was a little puzzled as to how she should address the class. Always before it had been, "Now, children." After I arrived she decided upon, "Now children, and you too, Mr. Tucker."

The Lord put me through a real period of testing in that class. My little classmates took great delight in tapping on the artificial appliance as I sat there in the cramped back seat, towering like a giraffe over the heads of others.

The teacher announced we would start by studying the parts of speech—nouns, pronouns, adjectives, and the like. With my background, I didn't know if such things walked or flew, but the dear saint of a teacher was long-suffering with me. She worked away at the rough edges with patience and understanding. One day, after about six months, she advanced the hope that a miner named Tucker might be salvaged after all.

Bright spots for me in the classroom labors came when the teacher had the children go to the blackboard. To get choice spots, they would dash up as if electricity had been applied. I didn't have to worry about where they wrote on the board. Plenty of room was left for me to write over their heads.

After a period of training, the teacher said we would have an examination. All the children wrote furiously, took their papers to the desk and left the room. A great battle was being fought on a rear seat. I was paralyzed with indecisions. Even my good hand wouldn't work.

Satan was working overtime. He said:

"Tucker, miner 602, why don't you give up? Go home and forget about this sentimental ministerial stuff. You've had enough embarrassment. Your place is back in a mining town, not in a cultured college city."

I was soundly whipped as I sat there, feeling sorry for myself, and was only moments away from packing my belongings for home. My heart cried out to God, "Lord, did you mean it when you said 'I will make you a fisher of men'?"

He meant it. The Christian teacher was used to turn defeat into victory. She walked back to the seat and asked, "Park, what is wrong?"

"It's hopeless for me to remember all the things you have taught us," I voiced.

"Bow your head," she commanded, "we're going to pray."

A quiet courage and renewal of determination came as we prayed in the lonely schoolroom.

"Now you answer the questions, Park, and I'll record them," she said.

When we finished, she corrected the paper and said, "You made ninety."

My glowing face would have made a lighthouse look like a candle. I went out of the room singing the praises of the Lord.

I had a sacred promise from God for the rough times "I will make you. . . ."

After nine months, I was promoted to high school

and things were different. The children came up to my waist.

Latin was my first great mystery in this new phase of higher learning. I had barely settled in the seat when the teacher said "Hic, haec, hoc." There was some question in my mind whether she was stuttering or trying to sneeze. Then, in language I could understand, she said, "For diversion, tomorrow we will have the numerals in Latin. Everyone study hard and have a good recitation."

I tried to study that night, but couldn't make sense out of the lesson and fell asleep.

Next day the teacher pointed her finger at me and said, "Mr. Tucker, will you please recite the numerals from one to ten?"

I didn't know the first one. As she waited, my mind flashed back to an Italian assistant during mining days. We had a sort of game of greeting each other and counting our pay checks in his language. And I remembered he had once told me that Italian and Latin were almost the same.

The teacher was still waiting, so I decided to give the numerals in Italian and see if she knew the difference. After I had finished, she said, "Brush up a little and you'll do fine."

Years later, I met Angelo on the street of Pittston and thanked him for his help in Latin class.

The academy instilled more than classroom subjects in me. I learned the meaning of the Scripture passage,

"Whosoever therefore shall confess me before men, him will I confess also before my Father which is in heaven." I had been leery of people who did a lot of talking about religion, but the passage showed me I was to be God's witness on earth. Such things may sound simple to others, but they were a revelation to me.

I began to give my testimony at the school, in the church, on the street and in my correspondence. God had begun to make use of the covenant I had made with Him.

The studies came easier and my days were filled with opportunities to witness. Leaves dropped off the calendar, until one beautiful June day in 1936 I walked across the platform with my little graduation classmates.

A titter ran through the audience. I was twenty-seven and the others were sixteen or seventeen. But the titters didn't worry me any more. My heart was filled with gratitude for the second chance God had granted.

The warmest moments came when I took the diploma home to mother and father. We gathered in the front room where I had been a patient so long. On our knees we thanked God for saving my life in the underground tomb and making it possible for me to begin my education anew at Wheaton.

The insurance benefits had been used, and I prayed another prayer before rising:

"Lord, will it be possible for me to go to a university or college, that I might literally show myself approved unto God as a workman that needeth not be ashamed, rightly dividing the Word of truth? Lord, it says in Scripture that You own the cattle on a thousand hills and that the gold and silver are Yours. If You can spare just a little bit, I would like to continue in school."

I prayed the same prayer all summer.

FAITH GOES TO COLLEGE

THE OLD DEVIL seemingly did everything he could to keep me from going to college. Father was suffering from his years in the mine. Mother was aging. The depression was at its height.

I received a letter from the registrar at Houghton College saying, "You should bring $355 if you come here."

My faith didn't quite come up to mustard seed proportions, but I informed him I would be there at the end of summer.

On my knees, I said, "Lord, I don't have thirty-five cents, let alone $355."

During the vacation period I obtained a very dignified

position as manager of the city dump. Members of my home church would drive up, open the car door, and hand me a basket of decaying food. Then, with a stunned look, someone would gasp, "Park Tucker, I thought you were a ministerial student."

Pretending to ignore the fragrant odors, I explained that it took money to prepare for the ministry. The church probably would have aided me financially, but a short time before it had donated large amounts of money to another young member for his ministerial education. Each summer he would saunter around town in his black suit, black tie and black shoes, contrasting with the golden cross upon his watch chain. But he had nothing of the Lord's calling within his heart. He told me later that he thought it was an easy way to get an education.

During the long days at the city dump, I found it was possible to commune with the Lord anywhere—even while sitting on an old box, watching the rats, smelling the stench and choking on the burning refuse at the foot of the dump. I had a library there, too. Fifteen Bibles were recovered from the trash. They were thrown away by some of the most prominent people in town. Such acts were typical of their lives. They had discarded God. Later, when war clouds came over the nation, they scampered for their Bibles and hymn books to stand up in a great chorus and sing "God Bless America."

Practically all of the money I received for working at the city dump had to be used in helping my parents and myself pay for the necessities of life. About one week before it was time to enter the college, I almost gave up the ghost. My savings were so small, and I again cried out to God, "How shall I ever get to go?"

The Lord hadn't forgotten. He was testing me to see how badly I wanted to attend college.

Six days before my scheduled departure, I used up a little more faith by telling my friends I would be leaving for college soon. Mother and father tried to console me as I became more desperate with each passing day. They said God's will would be done and reminded me that "... all things work together for good to them that love God" (Romans 8:28).

On Saturday morning, before I was to leave on Monday, I was on the way to the kitchen after morning prayer. The door bell rang. The postman was there. He said, "Park, here is a registered letter from Scotland for you. Sign your name."

I took the letter into the front room. The cheap Manila envelope was postmarked "Glasgow," "London," "New York City," "Scranton" and "Pittston." Mother and father, being discerning Christians, said, "Let's get on our knees; it is the answer to prayer."

We thanked God for answering our prayers before the letter was opened. A little blue piece of paper fell to the floor when I broke the seal. I picked it up and saw the hand of God in a twentieth-century miracle. The paper said, "Pay to the order of Park Tucker seventy pounds." It was drawn on the Bank of Glasgow. The pound at that time was worth five dollars. With

PRISON IS MY PARISH

the joy of the Lord in my heart, but with a touch of materialism, I figured that five times seventy was $350. The registrar had instructed me to bring $355. Like Peter of old, I cried, "Oh, Lord, that is just five dollars short."

As I was telling God's bookkeepers they had made a five-dollar mistake, my aged father put his hand into his pocket and pulled out an old crinkled five-dollar bill. He placed it on top of the seventy pounds.

The money had come from an old family inheritance that was being divided among the heirs. God had known way back then about the crippled coal miner who wanted to go to college and be a preacher.

I left for Houghton, New York, on schedule. From the first day, I tried to be a student pleasing to the Lord. I was still much older than the average student, but this didn't embarrass me any more.

After attending the college for a number of months, I received an invitation to be supply pastor of the nearby Baptist church. This was another big test from God. The town was named for David Hume, noted empiricist (who attributed the origin of all knowledge to experience). It was also the town of Bob Ingersoll, the famed agnostic. With such examples to follow, the people were very materialistic and had little time for God. I saw people buried in the earth without a word of prayer or Scripture.

Only seven people attended the Baptist church. Each Sunday I would stand forth like a John Calvin and preach the Gospel of the Lord to them. All seven would

THE BOY'S MOTHER WILL GET A BIRTHDAY CARD—WITH THE
AID OF THE CHAPLAIN AND A CHURCH "OUTSIDE."

I what do you mean boy I see a man

STUDENT TUCKER AND INSTRUCTOR DAVE TURNER TALK OF TAKE-OFFS AND TAILSPINS—

sit on one side of the church one Sunday and I would have them shift across the aisle on the following Sunday. I didn't want to become a right- or left-handed preacher. After much working and praying, the congregation increased to about fifty and we painted the church— the first time it had been painted in fifty years.

The following year I was called to the East Bethany Presbyterian church. John McGregor, then a young theological student and now a chaplain in the armed forces, went out with me for the first service. I don't believe any missionary in darkest Africa ever felt more disillusioned than John and I when we pulled off to the side of the road and looked at the pitiful church.

Graves of soldiers who died in the Revolutionary War were in the church cemetery. All were overgrown with grass.

God laid it on my heart to do what I could in rehabilitating the church. The first big job was to cut the grass. A regular lawn mower couldn't do the job, but a farmer agreed to come in with his big equipment.

The interior of the church was almost as bad. It hadn't been painted in more than twenty-five years. One Sunday morning, after preaching the sermon to about twenty people, I walked behind the pulpit without a word of explanation and tore the entire rear section of paper from the wall. Along with the crumbling plaster, it fell with a thud. Dust scattered over the shocked congregation. Then I announced that we would gather next morning to clean up the House of God.

The people realized they couldn't have church there

the next Sunday unless they worked. And they worked hard—with paper and paint on the walls, ceiling, pews and floor. They even painted the outside. Another problem was re-housing a large colony of bees from their church home of many years.

One of the old parishioners told me that when he was a young boy he often heard the bell ringing from the church belfry. I went up into the tower a few days later and discovered why the bell hadn't rung for so long. Pigeons had made their home there and the bell was caked. It wouldn't budge. More than thirty bushels of manure were hauled away. The bell was scraped, re-rigged and a new rope was attached.

On Sunday morning at ten-thirty the entire community was shocked when the bell pealed out its call for worship.

The Lord provided much fruit for our efforts at the little church.

My work continued at Houghton and life was good. But there came a day I had dreaded to see. It came only a short time after I had enjoyed a thrilling opportunity of holding a week's revival with other college students in my home town. Mother and father were there. They were so proud. But I could see that father was losing ground and would soon be called home.

He and mother were standing on the porch, with tears in their eyes, waving, when I left for college again. The last thing he said was, "Son, if I don't see you again on this earth, I will see you some day in heaven." I remembered the YMCA worker who had stopped him on the street the Sunday he was headed for a saloon. And I remembered the wonderful God who had breathed new life into me as I lay buried in the mine.

I had just returned to school when I received word that father had died. It hurt, but I knew in my heart I would see him again. I wouldn't trade this assurance for every dollar that has ever been printed.

Eleven months later, mother, too, went to be with the Lord. God gave me the privilege of standing by her bed and hearing her say, "Oh, Lord, let earthly trouble cease and call Thy servant home in peace." She had looked forward to this day, even though she hated to leave me behind.

Mother was the greatest missionary I ever knew. She prayed many years for her four girls. All were saved. She prayed for her prodigal son. It seemed that her prayers were not to be answered, but she never thought of giving up. She was sitting in the kitchen on the fateful Saturday afternoon, with my favorite food cooked, when the messenger came from the mine. She dropped to her knees, not knowing that God had already saved my life in answer to her faithful prayers.

Mother's prayers lifted me from the gruesome death of a lost miner to the thrilling, joyful life of a prison chaplain.

A Christian mother is the greatest asset on the face of God's wonderful earth!

A HANDSHAKE FOR
THE BRIDE

$\mathbf{M}$Y SOCIAL LIFE, for a long time, had been held back by the fear that the false arm and hand might be repulsive to girls. But I got the fear somewhat under control before leaving Wheaton and had a few dates, of the nonserious variety.

During my first year at Houghton I met a young lady who had transferred from Wheaton also. Her name was Margaret Smith. Margaret said she had called me once back at Wheaton and asked if she could ride in my car, along with several other students, on a planned trip to Scranton, Pennsylvania. She had relatives there.

I had bought an old automobile and used it as kind

of a taxi to help pay expenses. Margaret reminded me that I had refused her request and had told her six young men were going along.

That was about the only time I ever refused her anything. She later became my wife.

We became good friends at Houghton, but I was lined up kind of steady with another fine Christian girl. Margaret was usually along in the group that took part in testimony meetings and other campus activities. The more I saw of her, the less I seemed to be attracted to the other girl.

I was sitting in the parlor of the girls' dormitory one day doing a little idle chatting when Margaret walked by.

"Would you like to go for a stroll?" I asked.

We walked past the point, down by the creek and over to the pine trees at the edge of the campus. Sitting there, I realized for the first time that this was the girl I loved. A family of deer walked past. The buck, doe and young deer looked us over without the slightest trace of fear. What a beautiful family picture, I thought.

My dear was beautiful, too, and I wanted to tell her I loved her, but my mouth wouldn't cooperate. I was speechless. I tried to cover the appliance that served for an arm.

Then I got up enough nerve to whisper, "There is something I would like to tell you, Margaret."

She waited for a minute before replying, "Well, what is it?"

"I can't speak it," I said, "but maybe I can spell it. It starts with an 'L'."

She had a twinkle in her lovely eyes and smiled. "Could the next letter be 'O'?"

"Yes," I said, "and the next letter is 'V'."

She added, "Most likely the last one is 'E'."

Perspiration was pouring off my brow. It was the hardest spelling test I had ever taken, and the most thrilling.

This was about the only time Margaret ever showed poor judgment. She accepted my proposal. The wedding was to come later, after we had finished Houghton.

Ever since that day by the creek, however, Margaret and I have had a code in our mail. Friends often wondered why I signed my letters "LV" and why she used "OE." It took both of us to spell "love."

Margaret finished school one year before I did. She went home and spent the year teaching school, but came back with my sisters for the graduation.

The dean presented me with two tickets for my parents to attend the graduation. Handing them back, I said, "Sir, I won't need these. My mother and father have their own special seats."

He replied, "They will have to use these, as all seats will be reserved."

I answered, "Sir, I am not trying to be funny. My mother and father have gone to be with the Lord, and they are looking down at this graduation from the ramparts of heaven."

I worked hard that summer at the church I was

serving in East Bethany. The people were wonderful. They knew I was to be married in August and prepared a big party for us. Margaret came up on the Lehigh Valley Railroad.

The congregation presented her with something she had always wanted—an electric sewing machine. She had a real talent for sewing. I often marveled at the ingenuity she displayed to stay well dressed. She had a coat when she came to school as a freshman. I saw the coat as it gradually evolved to a jacket the next year, and to a muff and hat the next. God had given her talented hands to go with a good heart.

For months before the marriage I bragged, sometimes openly, about the great big kiss I was going to give Margaret when the minister pronounced us man and wife. She has laughed many times since about her "big lover." I don't remember exactly what happened, but she said instead of kissing her I turned around and shook her hand.

Margaret has been a perfect wife and wonderful mother of our two children. But she didn't stop there. Once, when I was pastoring a small church in addition to my prison duties, I couldn't get out of bed on Sunday morning because of a cold virus. She responded like a minute-woman. After doctoring me up, she grabbed her Bible, put the children into the car and drove thirty-five miles to the church, where she led the singing and preached the sermon.

When I reached the pulpit the following Sunday a deacon arose and said, "Brother Tucker, we will be very happy to have Mrs. Tucker take your place any time."

It was a fine tribute to my wife, but I have never been quite sure just how much of a compliment it was for me.

After our marriage, I made application to enter Eastern Baptist Theological Seminary in Philadelphia. The seminary replied that my application was rejected and that I should look elsewhere for my theological education.

Margaret was going to teach school in Chester, her home town, and it had been our prayer that I could attend the nearby seminary. Another reason I wanted to go there was because a conservative type of theology was taught.

We were puzzled about the rejection. I was ready to go elsewhere, but my wife was a go-getter. She said we would talk with the committee.

Dr. James Maxwell, a man I later discovered to be one of God's great heroes, expressed an interest in my case.

He said, "The committee has noticed from your application that you traveled around quite a bit, giving your testimony, and pastoring a number of churches." He explained that the committee, noting my advanced age, looked on me as an unstable person because I served in a number of different places.

I replied that I traveled wherever possible to take advantage of the opportunities offered by God.

Suddenly, Dr. Maxwell looked at me and said, "Mr. Tucker, they tell me you used to be a coal miner."

"Yes, that's right. God saved me in the coal fields," I replied.

God seemed to crack the case wide open here.

"As far as I am concerned," said Dr. Maxwell, "you can be a student at Eastern Baptist Seminary."

He was my steadfast friend all during my years at Eastern. Any student there who failed to know Dr. Maxwell missed a large part of his education.

During my senior year the Japanese bombed Pearl Harbor. I made application to become a chaplain in the armed forces. Many of my friends did the same. The services replied they didn't need men with one arm.

Margaret and I rolled with the blow and continued to serve God in any way we could. We had to be overcomers. She was my left arm—and no man ever had a better one.

PULPIT TO COCKPIT
AND VICE VERSA

A FTER GRADUATION, one of my classmates, William Caudill of Huntington, West Virginia, recommended me for the pastorate of the Tabernacle Baptist Church in Chillicothe, Ohio.

This was to be the city where God called me into prison work, but such a field of service had never entered my mind when I made the uneasy visit to be looked over by the congregation. I preached five times in a week and returned home. The congregation decided half a preacher was better than none at all. I was called to be full-time pastor.

I had served other churches before, but now I was

in the big leagues—on my first assignment after completing seminary studies. One of the outstanding evangelical preachers of Ohio had served the church before I was called.

God sent a gracious man to help me through the early testings and trials there. His name was A. T. Woodside, but to Margaret and me he was just "Woody." A man with a sharp brain, Woody ran the gamut of sin before finding Christ. He was a retired lawyer, working full time for the Lord.

In every church, I suppose, there are people who make a deep impression on the pastor, while others never get below the surface. Woody was the deep kind. Two others were Frank Meyers and Dane Turner.

Frank was a big, brawny, jovial railroad engineer. Friends said he had "spent enough money on liquor to start two or three churches."

For more than thirty years he was engineer and fireman on the Baltimore & Ohio running out of the terminal at Chillicothe to Parkersburg, West Virginia, and from Chillicothe to Cincinnati.

I first saw him as he stood ready to mount a B & O cab, when I was drawn to the area by an accident involving a railroad employee. Introducing myself, I offered to assist in any way possible. Frank said there were too many busybodies getting in the way already.

The rebuff aroused my interest. I inquired about his name and residence. It developed that he lived only three houses from my parsonage. Friends said he had no interest in churches or religion.

But God has many ways to make a man stop and think. Several weeks later this seemingly healthy engineer was forced into the hospital by internal hemorrhaging of some kind. While recuperating at home, he would walk by my house occasionally. He came by one day while I was sitting on the porch.

I smiled and greeted him by name. He came over and sat down, probably out of curiosity to discover how I knew his name. For a brief period in life, I had worked as a fireman on the Lehigh Valley Railroad and was able to speak his language. I gave him an account of my wanderings and personal history. He regarded it only as a good human interest story, but seemed to be impressed with the testimony of my salvation.

The time seemed right to ask, "Are you a Christian, Frank?"

He said he was a church member and had been baptized as a boy.

I repeated the question.

He replied, "My father and mother built a church out in the country."

"That's fine, Frank," I continued, "but I know many Baptists, Methodists and Presbyterians who are on the way to hell because they have never received Christ as Lord of their lives."

Finally, after a period of silence, he said, "Reverend Tucker, I don't believe I am a Christian."

I told him the wonderful plan of salvation provided by God and then asked if he would kneel in prayer. As we prayed, Frank found peace with God.

Frank began to grow in grace immediately. He regained his health and returned to the railroad run. He had been known as "Gabby" around the yards and shops. God didn't stop him from talking. He just switched the subjects.

He enjoyed a few delightful years after becoming a Christian. One day he brought in *The Diplomat,* a big fifty Pullman, and went home for his bath. Then he laid down on the bed—and died.

When I think of Frank, I remember a chorus he sang and hummed on the line. It went like this:

> Life is like a mountain railway,
> With an engineer that's brave;
> We must make the run successful,
> From the cradle to the grave;
> Watch the curves, the fills, the tunnels,
> Never falter, never quail;
> Keep your hand upon the throttle,
> And your eyes upon the rail.
> Blessed Saviour, Thou wilt guide us,
> Till we reach that blissful shore,
> Where the angels wait to join us
> In Thy praise forever more!

When one saint departed, another arrived.

All of us at Tabernacle Baptist rejoiced as the young men began returning from World War II. One Sunday morning an usher came to my study and said another of the lads was back. I walked out and was introduced to Dane Turner, an Air Force officer, and his wife. It was the beginning of a lovely friendship.

A few days later, Dane, who had piloted a B-29, came

to my office and told me of his dream to establish an airport in the city. It was a tremendous dream for a serviceman with only a small amount of money. We prayed about it and Dane decided to go ahead. He contacted an aircraft company and purchased his first ship. A farm was picked out for the airport site.

Dane became manager and flight instructor. The project seemed blessed. Flying became very popular in the city. He worked long hours.

A few months later his wife came to my office with tears in her eyes. She said, "Dane's traveling with the wrong crowd; please do what you can to help him."

Next day, I went out to the airport. Dane was standing on the wheel of a plane, measuring the gasoline in one of the tanks.

After we had exchanged greetings, he asked, "Want to take a ride in an airplane?" I probably fooled him by accepting. I told him about the courses I had read on how to fly an airplane. When he had sufficient altitude and the plane was level, he turned the controls over to me.

Only the Lord knew it at that moment, but He was about to change a pilot into a preacher and a preacher into a pilot. That's what came about.

It was my hope and prayer that the young man who once commanded one of Uncle Sam's million-dollar planes would go into full-time service for God, but I didn't pressure him. The change came about gradually.

One day, Dane walked down the aisle and surrendered his life to God. He left the airport and attended the University of Ohio, then Houghton College and Eastern Baptist Theological Seminary. Moreland Baptist Church near Muncie, Pennsylvania, called him to be pastor.

But before all this happened, Dane helped carry out the other part of God's plan. He taught me to fly, and it was no easy task, since I had only one hand to control the ship. Another friend designed an extension and handle on the throttle for me.

By the grace of the Lord and the patience of my instructor, I successfully completed the course. One of the highlights of my life came when I received the Civil Aeronautics Administration's private pilot license. Apparently, it was the only one of its kind—authorization for a one-handed minister to fly.

Many of the members of my congregation were a little upset about the dangers of flying, however. Some of the hair-raising events that were to follow showed their uneasiness was not farfetched.

HAND OF GOD

WE WERE HAVING a little bull session out at the airport one day when a friend remarked, "Reverend Tucker, you should have an airplane to help you get around faster."

"Sure would be great," I said, "but a plane on my salary is impossible."

Then Dane quoted a Scripture, ". . . with God all things are possible." He had planted a seed and given me cause to think. Sometimes it takes a new person in Christ to remind older ones of God's promises.

That night I prayed about it. I couldn't pray selfishly, asking God for a plane in which to ride around and have fun, but I did ask Him to help me get a plane if it could be used in His work. Two weeks later my good friend, Woody, asked me to ride with him about thirty-five miles toward Cincinnati to visit an abandoned church. At New Vienna we left the car and walked through high weeds to the building. The windows were smashed. The door was broken down and the pews were turned over. My heart ached as I stood before the filthy altar of God and saw the torn Bible—things that should have been more sacred to a congregation of church members.

Woody and I fell to our knees. We prayed that this church might be raised up again and ring with joyful music for the glory of God.

Two families were found, who had once been members of the church. We called a meeting of the families and their friends for a Monday evening and explained our intentions. They were interested. And they told us something rather startling. The church had a treasury of $5,000. This may have been the reason the church died. The money should have been in service for God. It had been lying idle, drawing interest, as the church dwindled away.

Woody took some of the money out of the bank and put it to work. We gave the church a thorough refinishing job. The building was soon ready and the people were anxious to begin worship services. They asked if it would be possible for me to preach regularly for them, along with serving my own congregation. The only way this could be done was with an airplane.

Dane was briefed on the situation and we decided to visit the Aeronca Aircraft factory at Middletown, Ohio.

113

The place was humming. Thousands of planes were being built to keep pace with the number of ex-servicemen taking aviation courses under the GI Bill of Rights. After touring the plant, we were taken into the president's office.

He seemed interested in the fact that I was a flying minister with one hand, but lost interest fast when he learned I wanted a plane and wasn't exactly loaded with money. In fact, he was a little indignant.

Said the president:

"Mr. Tucker, every plane on the line and every plane to be built next year is already paid for. It would be an impossibility for me to promise you an airplane—at full price."

There was that word "impossible" again. God must shudder every time He hears it. I looked at the president, but all I could think of was the little church at New Vienna, where neglect had left the dirty pulpit and torn Bible. God seemed to take over in the president's office. I said, "Sir, do you realize that the Aeronca factory, in its history of making airplanes, has built them for only two reasons?"

The president replied, "What do you mean, Reverend?"

I continued, "Every plane ever built on your line has either been used for the destruction of mankind or for financial gain. Don't you think that the big Aeronca factory could make just one plane for Almighty God?"

The president blinked. He was of the Jewish faith and believed in God. He whispered something to one of his aides and then asked if we could wait outside for a few minutes. When he called us back he said, "Reverend Tucker, we of the Aeronca factory are very happy not only to let you have the next airplane that comes off the line for Almighty God, but we will let you have it wholesale with the compliments of the factory."

I thanked him warmly and walked out.

"Wasn't that a real break?" said Dane.

"That was not a break," I replied. "That was the hand of God!"

In two weeks the plane was ready for delivery and I looked on as the test pilot wrung it out. He signed the approval form and I gave the officials a check. With a full tank of gasoline, I taxied out and gave it the gun for Chillicothe. A short while later we repainted the plane white and red. On the cowling we drew the insignia of Christianity, the cross and the crown.

The ship was pushed down the main street of Chillicothe and placed beside the church. At the evening service "The Evangel" was dedicated to the service of God. The benediction was given by a Reverend Long, then eighty-two years old. He had spent days covering the same route by horse and buggy that I was about to cover in a matter of hours.

On Sunday morning, after church service at Tabernacle Baptist Church in Chillicothe, I took off and flew at five thousand feet—no hands. Had to use my one good hand to eat a sandwich. Minutes later I was over New Vienna and buzzed the main street to let the people know the preacher had arrived, then landed in a nearby field. An ex-Navy man who had served on an aircraft carrier, stood on the railing of a fence and waved me in. No fighter pilot ever felt bigger than I did.

A waiting car took me to the church. I was amazed to see a huge congregation. The interest of the people had been aroused and the revived church, praise the Lord, was on its way.

The Evangel was faithful on long trips, too, when I was invited for speaking engagements. But there were many anxious moments when I would have been a goner without my wonderful Co-Pilot.

My license didn't authorize instrument flying, so I always tried to keep the ground in sight in order to use landmarks. Sometimes, however, things didn't go according to plan. The weather closed in on me fast one evening as I neared Cleveland for a speaking affair and I was lost in the "soup" at three thousand feet. I climbed to four thousand into bright sunlight, but there was no break to be seen in the cloud formation.

Three times I pointed the plane's nose into the fog and held my breath down to eight hundred feet without finding a break. The gas gauge was resting on zero. Any moment I expected the engine to sputter, cough and die. A crackup and death seemed inevitable.

The wind drift was carrying me toward the Great Lakes. As far as I knew, I could have been over water at the time. My stomach seemed to be tied in knots.

Inwardly, I cried out to God:

"Oh, Lord, the children of Israel saw the enemy to their rear and the sea in front. You delivered them.

Please help me! I am thousands of feet in Your sky; I'm on a journey for You; I'm to preach Your Gospel, and this is Your plane. Oh, Lord, place the wheels on the solid runway of an airport. In Christ's name. Amen."

I lowered the nose. In the steep glide the altimeter dropped quickly—4,000 . . . 3,500 . . . 3,000 . . . 2,500 . . . 2,000 . . . still nothing but clouds . . . 1,500 . . . I cried out, "Oh, Lord, help" . . . the clouds parted just like the waters of the Red Sea. Directly below were the concrete strips of the huge Cleveland airport. There was no gas for circling, so I went straight in. As I reached the apron a voice from the tower came over the radio, "84227, we didn't see you land; 84227, we didn't see you land." I took off my flying cap, wet with perspiration, and bowed my head in a thankful prayer, "Lord, they didn't see me land, but You sure did."

I felt a new vitality that night in the Youth for Christ service, and the Lord greatly blessed.

Next morning The Evangel's engine purred after the Cleveland take-off for the return trip to Chillicothe. Lazily, I watched the farms and rivers unfold below. Suddenly, the dreaded fog closed in again. I flew low, hunting an airport, but failed to locate one. The fog thickened. I picked out a farmer's field and came in low over his house. There was no tower operator to miss my landing, but an old cow lifted her head, sleepily, and watched me bump to a halt in a corner of the field.

My service at Chillicothe was to be at ten-thirty. It was an hour before the fog cleared. I spent the time in further study and prayer for the morning message. The

117

take-off was successful, if bumpy, and I headed for home. My favorite navigation instruments, the C & O and N & W railroad tracks, showed up near Columbus and the rest was a breeze.

The organist started the prelude as I stepped into my church study. Some of the members probably thought I slept late as they speculated on the easy life of a minister. They didn't know that the mighty hand of God had swept clouds away and saved my life twice in less than twenty-four hours.

A routine flight to Cincinnati one day enabled me to be the guest speaker on Radio Station WLW's program, "A Church by the Side of the Road." It was the first time I had spoken on a 50,000-watt station that would reach tens of thousands all over the United States.

The message was entitled, "The Making of a Man." God works in mysterious ways. A week later I was contacted by a University of Cincinnati co-ed, who had a story to tell.

The girl said she was sitting on the side of her bed at eight o'clock on Sunday morning, after an all-night drinking orgy. She held a sewing needle in one hand and a thread in the other as she tried to focus her eyes and thread the needle. A button needed replacing before she went to sleep.

She had flipped on the radio when she came in. It was making her head ache, but she felt too bad to get up and turn it off. The needle and thread were given up as a hopeless cause.

A church program was announced on the radio. She

groaned. The subject was given, "Making of a Man." She giggled. This would be a great message for a girl.

There was nothing for her to do but listen as I attempted to portray the love and mercy of God, by which any man or woman, no matter how degraded, can have dignity restored. At the end of my concluding prayer, she fell on her knees at the side of the bed. She remembered her life as a young girl at home with a godly mother and how Sunday mornings were spent at church instead of trying to thread a needle after a drunken party. She asked God to have mercy on her.

On the same day that she heard the broadcast, the university dismissed her because of low grades and immorality. But God had given her new life and she was reinstated. Later she graduated and became an outstanding Sunday school teacher.

The young lady said she didn't know what might have happened in her life if she hadn't stayed awake trying to put a piece of thread through the eye of a needle.

COME OVER AND HELP

ONE AFTERNOON I was driving in the outskirts of Chillicothe on the way to Columbus when I passed the Federal Correctional Institution. I stopped and took a long look at the huge reservation. It resembled a college campus. Over eleven hundred young boys were locked up there because something had gone wrong in their lives. Many of them probably never had a chance.

As I continued to look, the Lord pricked my heart and I was filled with the realization that only the grace of God had prevented me from being an inmate of such an institution. Instead, blessings had been poured out in abundant measure.

It seemed, as I gazed across the barbed wire fence,

where guards with guns occupied strategic points, that I heard the same beckoning as Paul when he looked toward Macedonia . . . "Come over and help us."

God showed me that day my new field of service was to be behind walls in one of the twenty-six institutions of the Department of Justice. I made it a point to become friends with the chaplain at the Chillicothe institution and took what was called an "in service" training period of three months. Later a vacancy appeared in the chaplaincy corps and I made application for the post.

The assignment came soon afterwards, first full-time chaplain at the Federal Correctional Institution up in the hills near Ashland, Kentucky. The walls held four hundred men, most of whom had been caught while dealing in "moonshine" whisky.

It was hard to resign from my church in Chillicothe, but my call was from God.

A residence near the institution was not to be found. The closest was twenty-five miles away, across the Ohio River. I had to drive through parts of three states, Ohio, West Virginia, and Kentucky, to reach my work.

The Reverend William Caudill, a friend who had graduated in my seminary class, rented us a home for twenty-five dollars a month, but we still had a hard time making ends meet. My salary was much less than the one I received at Chillicothe. Close figuring showed that we had five dollars every two weeks for our food budget. This may seem startling, but God never allowed us to miss a meal. Sometimes, however, we glanced toward heaven to see if the ravens were going to bring it down.

The anxious periods may have been caused by the fact that God had made me into a two-hundred pound man with a hungry stomach.

Before my arrival, the chaplaincy at Ashland had been on a part-time basis, with local ministers alternating in holding services. My first job was to set up an office for consultations with prisoners. Then I bought the fittings for a chapel.

I made many mistakes in dealing with the men during the seventeen months of my service at Ashland, but God overruled my lack of experience and provided gracious friends to help me over the hump on hard days. My greatest asset, it seems, was that I was willing, and wanted so desperately to do an intelligent job of presenting the prisoners a new way of life.

It was at Ashland, also, that I was indoctrinated in the cunning ways of men behind bars. Dr. Janney made up cough syrup for the men during winter months, when colds were prevalent. It contained licorice, rock candy and a little codeine. The last ingredient made it very attractive to the men and they figured out a way to get it—without a prescription. They made connections with an inmate clerk. The syrup supply didn't recede unreasonably, but the strength was far lower toward the end of the month than when it was first made. The clerk added water to bring up the volume each time he pilfered some for the men.

Shortly after the end of my first year at Ashland, the warden gave me a communication stating that authorities in Washington, D. C., would like me to consider the position of chaplain at the Federal Penitentiary in Atlanta. I was a little frightened at the thought of leaving my four hundred "moonshiners" and working with some of the world's most notorious criminals.

After making the offer a matter of prayer, I flew to Atlanta and remained a week in looking over the situation. God did not burden me to take the post, so I turned it down. One of the factors in my decision was that it would have been almost impossible for my family to exist with the added expense of living in a big city. There was no home on the reservation for us.

I resumed my duties at Ashland, where Margaret and I, and daughter Lynelle, were very happy. The work continued to go forward as I gained new experience in the important field of service.

Six months later, I had another letter from Washington officials saying they would like to have me reconsider the Atlanta opportunity. This offer included a house on the reservation. Margaret and I again prayed about the matter. The house made it sound attractive, but this was not the reason we decided to accept. The decision came from God, who was providing the larger opportunity.

The time was near when Margaret was to give birth to another child. My son, Richard, was born about a month later. She took the children to the home of her parents in Philadelphia, where she could rest and regain her strength. The trucking concern left with our furniture, bound for Atlanta, and I stayed at Ashland waiting for a favorable weather report. There had been too many forced landings to take unnecessary chances.

During the few remaining days I roomed with a young doctor named Smith, who was from Texas. He did his time harder than the inmates. In his heart, he yearned for the tumbleweeds and cactus of Texas. Each morning he would get up and mark off one of the days on the calendar.

There was one belonging that had been left behind by the furniture van and I couldn't take it with me in the airplane. A graduate of Baylor University had given it to Margaret and me as a wedding present. It was a cactus that had grown to large proportions after being planted in Kentucky's fertile soil. I dug the cactus up and planted it outside the doctor's office late one night. A sign was placed alongside. It read, "Texas, 1,500 miles."

The doctor was on duty when I left, but he remembered the Alamo, no doubt, when he came in that night.

Taking off in The Evangel, I climbed to five thousand feet. The Ashland institution passed beneath the wings as I leveled off for the flight south. Memories crowded the cockpit.

I landed at Cartersville, Georgia, just north of Kennesaw Mountain near Atlanta, to refuel. It was a kind of shade-tree airport, with very little activity. A young flier said I would be better off for the night if I flew on over the mountains to Atlanta instead of staying in Cartersville. He meant well, but complications set in after the take-off. Darkness came along fast, before the mountains were cleared, and forced a landing. I approached a likely looking pasture and was letting down for the landing before noticing the contour farming pattern, with retaining walls to keep the land from washing away. And then I saw a large ditch. I put the controls down, gave it full throttle and applied the brakes. With the bouyancy of the blast of the propeller under the wings, the plane leaped from one lip of the ditch to the other. When the plane finally stopped, the propeller was within six inches of a barn on the side of the field.

An old farmer came out and said, "By golly, you almost wrecked that airplane."

I answered, with more steadiness than I felt, "Sir, this is the Lord's airplane."

"Another crazy aviator," he muttered, scratching his head.

Through his generosity, I stayed at the farm all night. Next morning, with the farmer and two hired hands, we moved the plane over to the corner of the field. The plane raced across the bumpy acres and made it into the air.

Atlanta showed up on the other side of the mountain. The Evangel seemed dwarfed by all the mighty airships parked at the terminal. And I felt almost as small and insignificant as I set out by taxi to be chaplain at one of the largest prisons in the world.

ONLY THE WOUNDED CAN SERVE

In atlanta, as at Ashland, I leveled with the men from the first day. They knew where I stood, and I tried hard each day to understand more about their problems.

Many people, especially students in colleges, universities and seminaries, have asked me what it takes to be a prison chaplain. The first requisite, of course, is being born again by the Spirit of God, but something else is needed for the specialized field of prison work. I believe Thornton Wilder summed it up with a sentence in his book, *The Angels that Troubled the Water*. He said, "In love's service, only the wounded can serve."

126

A man who has been wounded and has known sorrow is more capable of broad understanding.

In addition, someone once said a chaplain must have a hide like an alligator, a heart as big as a lion, the brain of a genius and be covered by God's grace. Few men, however, including Park Tucker, can meet those qualifications.

But I had been wounded. I knew the sorrows. I knew the temptations. And the prisoners soon knew as much about me as I knew about myself. They knew when I stood up on Sunday morning that I was giving them something more than information from textbooks.

One of their favorite talks, and one which was used by God to bring results, went like this:

"In the forty-second Psalm, we have a song that the ancient Hebrews sang when they were troubled and discouraged. Their deep feelings toward the blessings of God are revealed in the first verse. 'As the heart panteth after the water brooks, so panteth my soul after thee, O God.' It was their God and this song that gave them victory over their problems. God can do the same thing with an individual that He did for Israel. He can deliver you from your confinement.

"Many of you remember Forrest Turner as one of the most notorious criminals and escape artists in Georgia's history. I sat as prison chaplain one night and heard him tell how Christ had lifted him from the pit of a state penitentiary to a life of hope and joy.

"The only way you can arise from yourself, your sins and your confinement is by God's grace. You have tried

127

reasoning. You have tried studies and philosophies. All failed. Paul, who was a prisoner, had the answer. He said, '. . . if any man be in Christ, he is a new creature. . . .' Christ is the answer to your problems.

"But let me warn you of this. Many a man has missed the mark of peace of mind, peace of soul and the act of redemption because of just eighteen inches—eighteen inches between the head and the heart.

"A young man from the province of Georgia in Russia went to a theological school, read the Bible and recited prayers. The same man later in life destroyed those who loved God and the Bible. He was Joseph Stalin, a man who never had Christ in his heart. Inmates here can recite prayers, quote Scripture and hang religious decorations around their necks, but few can say with Paul, 'For me to live is Christ, and to die is gain.'

"If you sincerely want to rise from your confinement, then cast your eyes upon Jesus; look full in His wonderful face, and the things of this earth will grow strangely dim in the light of His wonder and grace.

"So many of you men have told me of your secret desires. You have trained your bodies; you have trained your minds; you have given attention to every phase of your life, with the exception of the spiritual. It isn't any secret that you have tried to impress me with your knowledge, your brain power, your I.Q. All I could see as you talked was power, security, a fast buck, lay it on the line, brother. There wasn't a word from the heart—about mercy, charity, love of others and the kindnesses of life.

128

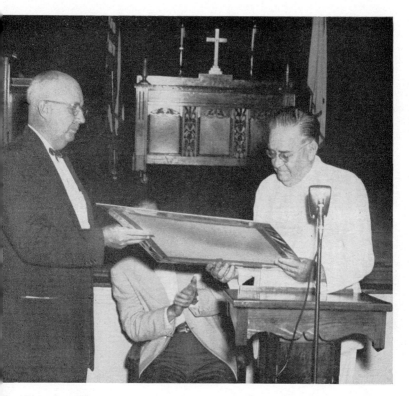

ATLANTA CITY MISSION PRESENTS A PLAQUE HONORING DR.
TUCKER FOR HIS PREACHING AT MISSION SERVICES.

RALPH EDWARDS AND THE TUCKERS ON "THIS IS YOUR LIFE"
—LOS ANGELES, MARCH 21, 1956.

"This is your day of opportunity. You must make a choice between the philosophies of the head and the heart. It's either the head—'I'm number one and everyone else can go to hell,' or the heart—'Come unto me, all ye that labour and are heavy laden, and I will give you rest.'

"As I stand behind this sacred desk and look into your faces, I often think of the man who wore the number 6156 on his Washington State Penitentiary uniform. As an immigrant, he entered the gangs of Chicago and later became a train robber. He was in the death house, counting the days, when he read the promises of Christ to anyone who would believe—even Michael Novak. Like Paul in the jail at Philippi, he called out and was saved. Old things passed away.

"Novak's death sentence was reduced and he was later completely exonerated. He prepared himself for the ministry and recently preached to you from this same pulpit. You saw him as he fell on his knees, with tears dropping from his eyes, and pleaded with God to help you.

"We can look back and see a Forrest Turner; a Michael Novak; Ralph Tetterman, the gangster of Chicago; Joseph Cellini, Anthony Zeolli and thousands of others who wore the uniform of an inmate before God dressed them up in sharp, new clothes.

"One day in the institution, I asked an inmate to give me a good theological analysis for the redemption of man. With a quick move of his hand, he took the Bible from my desk and opened it to the Scriptures. He said, 'I am a Christian because I have accepted—"behold, now is the accepted time. . . ." ' He then turned to another portion and said, 'I am a Christian because I believe—"Believe on the Lord Jesus Christ, and thou shalt be saved. . . ." ' With another turn he showed me the monumental Scripture, '. . . as many as received him, to them gave he power to become the sons of God. . . .'

"He added: 'Chaplain, it's just A.B.C.—accept, believe, confess.'

"The university and seminary have never offered a better analysis.

"And it worked for the man who gave it to me. I saw his face turn from that of a wicked moonshiner to the face of a man at peace with himself and God."

Another favorite with the inmates was the story of the Good Samaritan. One reason may have been that they had often been treated like the victim by the priests and levites of our world today.

This is one of the great tragedies of life—a man needing help, and people passing him by on the other side.

In talks with the men, I pointed out the three philosophies involved in the story.

The philosophy of the robbers was "What's yours is mine; I'll take it." We have had this type of person since the beginning of time. Cain told the first lie. Rachel was an example of grand larceny. The FBI reported 1,763,290 major crimes last year.

The philosophy of every thief who has ever lived has been the same—"Something for nothing."

Only a shade different was the philosophy of the priest and levite—"What's mine is mine; I'll keep it." The same kind of thinking is found today, both within and without the church.

A few years ago a Senate crime committee was investigating a well-known individual for his criminal activities. When asked what he had done for his country, he said, "I paid my income tax." What a statement from a man who has enjoyed the privileges of this nation. My classmate at seminary, Chaplain Kenneth Hyslop, went with our troops to Korea and never returned. The only message that came back said, "He was injured and starved to death." As Kenneth lay on a frozen road in Korea, with the shiny cross pinned to his dirty shirt, he didn't answer a Senate committee, but he could have said to the Lord, "I have loved my country; I have paid my taxes; I have given my life for others, but most of all I have tried in my simple way to be an ambassador for You."

Then, there was the philosophy of the Samaritan— "What's mine is ours; we'll share it."

In the huge city of Atlanta, with its hundreds of churches, one of the greatest sermons preached daily is from a little shoe-shine establishment run by a colored man. Every time I go near the place on Marietta street, I get my shoes shined whether they need it or not. It's a benediction to see the love of God sparkle through the dark skin and to read the words on his plaque: "Christ first, others second, self last." He is the good Samaritan.

When inmates heard the three philosophies explained, they had little trouble finding the slot into which they fitted. But no matter what the slot, they were always told about the one God would have them fill.

And many of them changed to a new way—"What's mine is ours; we'll share it."

"SOMETHING HAPPENED...
TO ME"

On walks around the prison yards and down through the cell corridors, where the locks clang shut every night on men jammed together from all corners of America and several foreign countries, I have talked with scores of prisoners who have discovered the answer to frustration and who have more peace of mind than thousands of wealthy people now roaming the world with complete freedom.

For the scoffers, who brush such things aside by saying "They are locked up and can't do anything wrong," I say, with all sincerity, don't you believe it. A man so inclined can cause a lot of trouble in prison. Bad actors are dealt with, firmly, but towering walls don't eliminate temptation and ingenious plans. Some may think the men play us for suckers and become Christians to get out. Christ doesn't shorten the sentence. He helps a man to live with it.

Let some of the men who have changed tell you what it is like, in their own words. I deserve no credit. It's not by might, not by power, not by a one-armed chaplain, but by My Spirit, saith the Lord.

When they ask questions, I try to give them the answers, in understandable language. People behind walls have a habit of wanting it that way, like the Philippian jailer who asked Paul, "What must I do to be saved?" And Paul answered, "Believe on the Lord Jesus Christ, and thou shalt be saved. . . ." What a straight question and answer exchange! A number of ministers today, seemingly, haven't learned this simple lesson. Someone has aptly said, "If the vogue for theological training had been as great in the first century as it is today, Paul would have had to answer the Philippian jailer in this manner—'Adjust yourself to the unconditional, bring being and non-being into balance and make a compulsive reorientation.' The building would have fallen on the jailer before he could have looked up the words in the dictionary."

Listen to Frank, who trafficked in "white slavery" and just about everything else that came across his sordid path:

"I can sit in my cell and look at the people in passing cars. Not long ago I was one of those people. I was a taxi driver, meeting every kind of person on earth.

"The best I met was one of the sweetest Christian girls in Marietta, Georgia, and it was easy to fall in love with her. She wouldn't have anything to do with me because of the way I was living, so I decided to act like I wanted to be a Christian. An act, nothing else. The girl judged me by the cover and consented to marriage. This was one of the last happy days she has had. When she saw what I really was, however, she prayed for me, faithfully.

"I began to twist some of her Scripture around. It told me to be fruitful and multiply. With the Bible on my side, I chased every woman I could find. I reminded myself that Christ changed water into wine, so it was okay for me to drink all the rotgut available. My wife prayed and Christian friends warned me I was on the road to hell. I told them I'd get right one of these days. No use to hurry.

"When Atlanta got too tame, I took off for the West Coast . . . drinking, fighting and living hilariously, thinking of no one but myself. I got a little broke and homesick before returning home. My wife forgave me and kept praying.

"I stayed around for awhile and left again. This time I went to Florida. While I was away, my wife gave birth to a son. Only God can forgive a man for deserting his wife at a time like that. I sent for her when she was well, and opened a little produce business. She worked for me until I took off without notice for Miami. Then she had to sell the business to get money for a return trip to Georgia.

"Once again I returned home and she forgave me. She still had faith. . . .

"I got a job at a gasoline station. On the job one day, I passed through the valley of the shadow of death. I had a heart attack! Operations were needed. Like most people, when no earthly person can help, I went to God. I prayed every day and made all kinds of promises, if He would only forgive and heal me. He did! Within two weeks, I was on my feet and feeling well. Soon I was out looking for another job.

"It wasn't long before I forgot all the promises and went back to the old life, only worse. I became a 'white slaver.' For those unfamiliar with the term, it is selling flesh for use in prostitution. The law caught up and sent me to prison. But the worldly prison could never be as bad as the spiritual prison in which I had placed myself.

"My wife continued to wait . . . and pray. She is still waiting.

"In prison I began to reason with myself. . . . If a Christian can be so forgiving after all I have done, surely our Creator can be even more forgiving. He said He would forgive us, not seven times, but seventy times seven. He defended the adultress about to be stoned to death by worldly leaders. He said '. . . though your sins be as scarlet, they shall be as white as snow. . . .'

"I enrolled in the Bible course started by Chaplain Tucker, to learn more about God's promises. Through the course, I began to learn the importance of humility and love for God and my fellow man. I attended church services and Sunday school. Through the 'everyday' language of Mr. Tucker, and the Spirit of God, I was moved to think through the sermons I heard each Sunday.

"Daily Bible reading and association with other men who profess Christianity led me closer to Him.

"My wife visited me as often as possible and wrote almost every day. Each letter was shining with the testimony of what God was doing for her and the children, and what He could do for me if I would only let Him. One evening as I read her letter in the quietness of my cell, it seemed as if the walls were closing in on me. Sweat began to trickle from my face. Nervously, I wanted to call for help, from someone. Inwardly, I cried, 'Lord, forgive me, just show me the way and I'll make it, with Your help.'

"A clean feeling came over me. I knew He had heard my prayer. And that this time I was going to keep my promises. That was ten months ago. I have helped organize Christians inside the walls to meet each evening in the prison yard for the study of God's Word and prayer for other prisoners.

"Today I stand beside bank robbers, dope peddlers, white slavers—all types—who sing with me the praises of God in the church choir of the penitentiary. All of us are aware there is no freedom, no security, no happiness, unless it comes through Jesus Christ.

"It may seem that I am like the Pharisee, who shouted

from the rooftops how righteous he was, but I hope the reader will take it as the publican, who humbly says, 'God forgive me, for I have sinned.' "

If nothing else had happened in my life, how could I doubt the power of God after knowing a man like Frank.

Listen to another. His name is Hugh.

"I have lived in filth for most of my twenty-four years. By the time I was twenty-one I had been charged with burglary, larceny, grand theft, unlawful flight to avoid prosecution, assault with intent to rob while armed, breaking and entering, forgery and fraud, theft of a motor vehicle by fraud, escape from jail, felonious assault on officers while attempting to escape, pandering, possession, sale and use of narcotics, carrying concealed weapons, kidnapping, possessing and stealing stolen property, and bank robbery. Doesn't seem to be much left.

"I had adopted the philosophy that 'the only way to advance in the world is with money.' And the only way to get money was by force. For getting it this way, at the age of eighteen, I was sentenced to three years probation, sixty days in the county jail and a fine of $250. This was followed, on another conviction, by an indeterminate sentence of six months to fifteen years in the state prison of southern Michigan at Jackson. Because of my age, I was transferred to Michigan State Reformatory at Ionia. After being released on parole, which I violated several times, I was caught again and given fifteen years at Leavenworth Penitentiary, with some twenty charges of armed robbery and miscellaneous counts awaiting my release from Federal custody.

"In Leavenworth I got into trouble and advanced a step closer to dreaded Alcatraz by being transferred to Atlanta. As I sat in the lonely cell of the Orientation Unit, with the next thirty or so years of my life promised to the Federal Government and the state of Michigan, and faced with three detainers for armed robbery carrying a maximum sentence of life imprisonment, I looked out at the wall and began to think for the first time in my life.

"What future did I have? What had I gained by my associations with pimps, prostitutes, numbers men, gamblers, bandits, con men, petty swindlers, safe crackers, bank robbers, crooked cops and assorted gangsters? What did life hold for me?

"I thought about my past. When my common-law wife was pregnant we had an argument that ended with me never seeing the son I fathered. It wasn't long afterwards that I was trapped into a legitimate marriage which produced another son. I couldn't escape responsibility.

"With the parole officer breathing down my neck at all hours of the day and night, I managed to provide a decent home for the family. But a house with four walls to keep out the cold and something to eat in the ice box, without understanding, do not make a home.

"My mother was highly excitable and my father was an alcoholic. My three brothers and sisters were in a children's home.

"This may explain part of my trouble, but the rest

139

of it was caused by the great 'I . . . I . . . I' that dominated my life. I abused my wife, callously. She was an ex-parolee from a state institution, but was sincerely trying to make life happy for our family. It was easy to use her as an outlet for my frustration.

"I tied up with some ex-cons and set out on a career of robberies which netted me nothing but headaches and a fifteen-year sentence. It was a hard effort to 'get the money and be somebody.'

"At the end of six months in Atlanta I was put into 'the hole' for fighting, while my mentally warped, bully opponent lay in pain in the prison infirmary.

"Unbathed for two weeks, I squinted my eyes against the warm Georgia sun when I was released from 'the hole.' What a dismal sight I must make, I thought. My weight had dropped to less than 125 pounds.

"Suddenly, there loomed before me a big man with a smile spread across his face. The wonders that lone smile did for me will never be captured on paper or in words. 'Hello, buddy, where have you been?' boomed the pleasant voice.

" 'In the hole,' I retorted.

" 'Well, that's too bad,' said the big man, 'but now that the ordeal is over, I hope you won't get involved again. What caused your trouble?'

" 'Just the explosive conditions brought on by my being crammed in an eight-man cell would be the real reason, I guess,' was the reply.

"The large voice continued, 'I know how it is being confined with seven other men day after day. I notice you have been attending services while you have been here. That is highly commendable. Do you attend because you are a Christian or just to get out of the cell?'

" 'A little of both, I guess, but I really enjoy church services,' was my honest reply.

"The big man added:

" 'Every Saturday we have fellowship meetings in my office. If you would like to get out for an hour or so on Saturday mornings, just drop a note to Chaplain Tucker and I'll send you a pass.'

"That was my first meeting with the chaplain. The next week I dropped word off in his office that I would like to be called out for Saturday meetings. Before the session began, he introduced me to a couple of young inmates and a couple not so young. I was asked to tell a little of my troubled past, if I had no objections. Before realizing it, I was up to my neck trying to explain my way out of irrational deeds.

"I will never forget how well my past errors were pointed out that day and how many good solutions were offered for my future improvement. Not all the suggestions came from Chaplain Tucker. Then, for some reason, I hurled a defiant, 'Well, the world owes me something, you know.' Mr. Tucker spoke in a quiet tone, 'Buddy, that can only be answered with a question. What have you to offer the world in return for what you receive?'

"I was transfixed! Couldn't even mumble a defensive evasion. I had absolutely nothing to say.

"After a long moment of silence, Mr. Tucker spoke

141

again. 'You feel, truly, that you have nothing, but you have many things. You have the ability to acquire a good education, the capacity to perform a day's work, a duty to love and tenderness for those who have great feelings for you. Above all, you have the responsibility of examining yourself and returning unto the world the harvest of teachings by Jesus, who said, "And as ye would that men should do to you, do ye also to them likewise." '

"The next day being Sunday, I noticed the sermon for the service was 'Examine Yourself.'

"I entered the chapel and heard the Reverend Tucker exhort members of the congregation to examine themselves before placing the blame on others. After thinking, hard, I determined never again to blame others for my faults.

"Today, three years later, my vision is clear, even though the road is rocky. I have found a new sense of values, peace of soul and the road to salvation through the guiding hand of God's man in these gray walls."

Can't you see in Hugh's life that nothing is impossible with God? When things appear hopeless, He provides hope.

Sam was a "paper hanger"—the underworld name for forgery. His story has an unusual twist:

"Now thirty-five years old, I had, previous to November 20, 1956, lived my life in constant turmoil from the age of thirteen. At that age I left home and started on the road to nowhere. I was never satisfied, always restless, always annoyed with everything and everybody. With that kind of life, it was only natural that I should wind up in the reform school, more than once, and then on to the penitentiary—five of them.

"I was wanted in seven states after being in four of the penitentiaries. On the lam as the result of a job, I was looking for a place to lay low, where the police and FBI couldn't find me. I went into a small mission in the Middle West under an assumed name and stayed there. But in order to stay, I had to attend the services each night and three times on Sunday. This went on for two months. The Scriptures truly state, 'So then faith cometh by hearing, and hearing by the word of God.' The Lord convicted me of my sins and I repented, with deep humility.

"After turning my life over to Christ and making peace with God, I had to make peace with the laws of my country, to the best of my ability, for crimes of forgery. I went to the FBI and other proper police authorities to reveal everything I had done. In every way possible, I cooperated to clear up the crimes for which I was wanted. Now I am serving my sentence in the Atlanta Penitentiary. There is also a detainer against me, but through all this Jesus has never left me comfortless.

"I have grown in wisdom, faith and strength . . . I have taken advantage of the rehabilitation activities made available here and know that when I have finished serving my time . . . Jesus will go with me and I will walk with Him.

"I am through with all things that Christ would not approve. . . . He means my hope for the future, not only in this earthly body, but in eternity.

"I am happy; I am contented; I am at peace with my God, and I am an inmate of the penitentiary. I praise Him from the depths of my heart."

Sam didn't leave any doubt as to whether he meant business. The perfect proof came when he gave himself up to the authorities in order to pay for his crimes. It cost him something. But it cost God something, too—the most precious possession He had, a Son, Jesus Christ. Would you sacrifice your son for a criminal?

Here's an inmate with the unusual name of Ise. He has a revealing story:

"I was so deep in crime in 1954 that I was actually relieved to enter prison. That may sound a little phony to some people, but it's true. Few people gain anything by stolen money. I would rather have $10 that I earned than $30,000 I had stolen.

"In July, 1954, I was in jail and prayed, 'Oh God, please deliver me from this jail.' I tried to make a deal with God by promising that if He would take me from the jail I would start going to church and do right. And I told Him that if I ever did wrong to put me back in jail.

"He sent a man I had never seen before to go on my bond.

"I started hitchhiking home that day and caught a ride, strangely enough, with two ministers. After arriving home at two o'clock the following morning, I couldn't sleep and went for a walk in a field near the house. I began to tremble and perspire. Feeling weak in the knees, I fell on my face, scared, but thankful to God for His help. I was still there, crying, when my wife found me. Words failed for several minutes. God had kept His part of the bargain.

"I failed!

"My wife wouldn't attend church with me and I had no religious friends. I went back to the same old road. God did His part again. Just as I had asked, He put me back into prison.

"My first six months were filled with bitterness and hatred. I couldn't sleep nights. I had chronic headaches, stomach trouble, sore feet, virus infection and sinus. One Sunday I went to a church service because a friend had been pleading with me for months. Chaplain Tucker talked on the ten lepers and how nine never thanked God for curing them. It seemed that the whole sermon was preached just to me. Reverend Tucker said, 'Let us be thankful for what God has done in our lives.' I began to think about what God had done for me. First, I thought of the deal I had made with Him some years back while in jail. Then, about how He had saved my life several times. It seemed as if I had been in His protecting hands all along without knowing it. That day I made a decision to have a talk with the chaplain and see just what could be done.

"I received a pass on Wednesday morning and went to his office. A man was there who knew God, an understanding man who was willing to listen. I told him the whole story.

"Then Reverend Tucker said, 'Christ is ready to forgive and forget.'

"We prayed. In the quiet office overlooking the walls, it seemed as if all the light in the world was shining. The place was radiant and warm. I vowed that day to become a new man.

"The following Sunday I had a front row seat when Reverend Tucker spoke. I stayed for Sunday school and then enrolled in the Bible course.

"When I pray now I don't ask for parole or early release. When God is ready for me to go free, He will open the gates."

Wouldn't it be wonderful if all church members in the free world had such an attitude?

Carl was typical of hundreds of car thieves who came to the penitentiary. Here's the way he tells it:

"I found myself sitting on a bed in the lonely cell. I was sick, disgusted, all mixed up within, full of despair and sadness—cut off from my loved ones, perhaps never to see them again. The future seemed like an eternity of blackness. Life had reached its limit . . . all I could think of was self-destruction.

"In this loneliness, I sat debating with myself. Into the Orientation Unit walked a man, Chaplain Tucker. He took an interest in me, re-awakened childhood memories of church, Sunday school and things of God. He told me where and why I fell . . . he told me I had to face reality.

"He asked me that day to read Philippians 3:13. I opened the pages of the little New Testament and read, 'Brethren, I count not myself to have apprehended: but this one thing I do, forgetting those things which are behind, and reaching forth unto those things which are before. . . .' Forgetting those things which are behind; reaching forth for what? What was ahead?

"God answered the questions. I felt Him pushing me to my knees. This was my chance for a new life. It was like a torrent pouring out. I longed to be forgiven, to know God, the living God. I hungered for Him and He gave me the desire of my heart.

"During the past twenty-six months I have been thankful for that day when I found God. . . . I can testify that He is as close to you as the air you breathe."

The Lord has never failed to honor His Word. I marvel at the power the Word shows everywhere—in top government circles, high society, city slums or behind walls.

Larry was a confidence man. Follow his incredible story:

"It seems like only yesterday when my mother and father were killed in an automobile accident. I was fifteen. We were not rich people and no estate of any kind was left. I had just finished the third year in high school and had to find a job. My parents had no brothers and sisters. Neither did I. There was no one close to help and my pride wouldn't allow me to ask others.

"I got a job in a grocery store as a stock clerk, working half the day and going to school the other half. My room in a cheap hotel cost $6 a week. It was here I met the people who became my friends.

"I met a fellow who worked on the Mississippi River as a deck hand. Mark Twain was one of my favorites. The river was my dream and this man was my hero. He was a drunkard and a spendthrift, but I admired him. When he said he could get me a job as a messboy on the boat where he worked, I quit school in the middle of my senior year and jumped at the offer.

"It didn't take long to find out the river wasn't all I had dreamed. The men were bums and hell raisers; the life was hard with little reward. I made four trips and quit the first time the boat docked at St. Louis.

"Foolish pride wouldn't allow me to return home unless I returned a big hero. It was war years and I decided to really do it up. I had saved a little money, a Coast Guard pass and Merchant Marine credentials, so I went to town and bought a fancy Merchant Marine officer's uniform before going home to see the girls.

"My bankroll disappeared quickly. I had seen people cash checks and had studied about them in school. Traveling to a bank in a town about fifty miles away, I deposited $50 in a checking account under the name Lt. Bill ————. The first check, of course, was for $50. Others came easy. In short order I wrote several hundred dollars worth of checks and was living it up. Soon I was dodging from one town to the next, writing checks, and staying one step ahead of the FBI. Then they caught up and I received my first time, a sentence of two years in the Federal Reformatory at El Reno, Oklahoma.

"While in El Reno, I completed my high-school education and looked forward to an honest life. Returning home eight months later on parole, I got a job as a bottle washer in a milk plant. The pay was forty cents an hour, five days a week. During the parole period I worked at various jobs—newspaper reporter, salesman, and factory worker, before marrying a home-town girl. It looked as if I were going to settle down and make something of myself. I was working as a sales engineer, earning about $200 a week and pushing toward a college degree at night school.

"Then lightning struck! I came home one night and found my wife with another man. I felt sick, lost, all alone. The feeling turned to disgust. The parole was completed and I was free. I joined the Army, but it didn't work out. Love for my wife still cut deep. I went AWOL to see her after being in the Army nine weeks. She was out on a date with another man. I returned to camp and was sentenced to ninety days of hard labor. Immediately after getting out of the stockade, I volunteered for the paratroopers at Fort Benning, Georgia.

"Once more I went AWOL to see her. This time the sentence was six months. After this was served I decided to settle down and be a good soldier. My wife consented to come to Fort Benning. It wasn't long before I found out she was running around with all the soldiers at the fort, so I sent her home.

"I was doing a poor job as a public relations reporter with the post newspaper when the Provost Marshal called me over one day and told me he had a letter from my wife saying I had a criminal record. I had failed to tell the Army about it. The policy forced my discharge for fraudulent enlistment.

"Disgusted, not knowing where to turn, and still in love with my wife, I forgot by drinking and traveling about the country as a salesman. Sometimes I sent the orders in; sometimes I pocketed the money.

"In Nebraska I was picked up by the law and sentenced to three years in the state penitentiary for taking money under false pretenses. During my stay in the institution, I received word that my wife had gotten a divorce and married again. Like a fool, I attempted to escape. They added another year to my time when I was caught several hours later. Finally the time was served and I had the equivalent of two years in college, plus many specialized courses from the International Correspondence School.

"My mind was made up. I was going straight. In Lincoln, Nebraska, people said jobs were scarce and wanted references. References I didn't have. The $20 given me when I left prison didn't last long. Broke and unable to find regular employment, I took a job selling Bibles for a mail-order house that didn't ask for references. All it wanted was sales. I sold my way to California, making about $30 a day selling Catholic and Protestant Bibles. On each sale my commission was $5. By the time California was reached, I had saved a few dollars, and found a wide-open field—where thousands of Mexican Catholics lived. Why should I get only $5 on a Bible when the company must be getting $10, I figured. So I found a company in Texas that made the Bibles and made arrangements, under the pretense that I was a big company, to have several thousand shipped to me on a consignment basis.

"The Bibles arrived and I hired people on straight commissions to sell. We used all kinds of tactics, selling to illiterates as well as literates. We took the last penny of many to pay for the 'big beautiful, red Bible' with all the pictures in it. Everything was going fine—until we saturated the state with Bibles. Then I convinced some local people that things were wonderful, and left the sinking business in their hands for several hundred dollars. I really gave them the business.

"Before they could get wise I started back east, spending and drinking along the way, and then headed for sunny Florida. Down in Georgia, I was in a diner when an officer checked my car for being in a no-parking zone. He asked if it was my car. It was. And he found a pistol in my glove compartment. To this I admitted ownership, since I carried large sums of money and needed protection. The reason wasn't acceptable and I was sentenced to ten months on the Georgia chain gang for having a pistol without a license. There was no one to take over the payments on my car and no one to store my clothes. I lost everything.

"Released from Georgia with no money, nowhere to go, no hopes, I had lost all faith in humanity and decided the only way to make a go of it was to steal my way through life. The plan was to take the country for what I could, while I could.

"The plan didn't last long enough, however. I was caught six months later by the FBI and given three and a half years to think things over in the Federal Penitentiary at Atlanta.

"This was my discouraging background as I sat in prison. It seemed there was to be no end to my capers. But something happened. I was given a job of responsibility and met the chaplain. He talked sense, and gave me a New Testament. As I read the Book I became interested in this Man who had walked the earth some 1900 years ago. I borrowed from the chaplain's personal library and read more about the Man they persecuted, the Man who had twelve friends, only to be betrayed by one of them.

"I prayed for help. It seemed that every time I left the chaplain's office I felt more secure, more sound, and I began to have more confidence in the guiding hand of Jesus Christ.

"When I changed, I don't know. It was a slow process. I began to realize that old things no longer appealed to me.

"A 'bum rap' caused me to lose my job of responsibility. But, wonder of wonders, I felt no bitterness toward him—only love. I actually prayed for someone else. After a few days of special confinement, I was placed on a construction detail.

"As I worked in the hot sun, I prayed to God for mercy, and understanding of my accusers. I worked on the detail for five months, along with all the alleged troublemakers. One day the associate warden came to me and asked if I would like to change jobs. I was assigned to be a clerk. Surely this was the hand of God. He had put me with the only real friend I had found. I was working in the office with the man who had led me to God.

"Now I could read, study and learn more about Him. Truly, God works in wondrous ways.

"I am still working, and I plan to do full-time work for the Lord some day when I am a free man. I shall let His will be done in my life."

Who can cast doubt on the straightforward, burning words of these prisoners, who ask for nothing except the right to love the Lord Jesus Christ? In the telling of their inspiring stories, it was necessary for them to mention my name, but I know you will see that all the glory must go to Christ. Park Tucker just happened to be on hand when God was at work.

The men will receive no self-glory from the telling. Such was not their intention. But, some day, I believe, they will hear from the lips of the Lord Himself how their unselfish words of truth penetrated prisons around the world and into the hearts of men without hope. The men in our prison don't know anything about theology, but they do know that something wonderful happened . . . to them.

We thank God for the privilege of telling others that in Him there is life . . . life everlasting.

FAREWELL TO THE EVANGEL

INVITATIONS FOR SPEAKING engagements began to come in from civic clubs and churches in the Atlanta area, mainly because some of our "graduates" were spreading the word around that God had an "unusual" one-armed servant as chaplain at the pen.

I accepted whenever possible. The covenant with God was that my life would always speak for Christ.

Rarely did I accept an engagement, however, without recalling my days under the teaching of Professor Stanley Wright at Houghton. He gave me the fundamentals on how to express myself as an ambassador for the Lord. It is a privilege for me just to include his name in this book. He dedicated his entire life to helping others. I doubt if he ever earned more than $3,000 a year for his ministry, but Professor Wright never evaluated his work in terms of silver and gold. His only concern was how much service he could give to the Master.

Years later, when I was called back to Houghton to address the student body, I looked down and saw him sitting in the front row. His hair was gray and age had taken its toll in other ways, but I caught the merry twinkle in his eye. There must have been a thousand times when he doubted whether I would ever be able to stumble through a speech.

It may have been that Professor Wright and God went to a little special trouble with me, because from the first until this day I have never given a talk, no matter what the circumstances, in which I didn't try to present Jesus Christ as the answer to man's problems.

Another policy I have kept is that no price shall be placed on my message to any organization. I have never asked for an honorarium and I have never asked an individual or organization to reimburse me for expenses. I am a firm believer that God takes care of His own. If expenses were offered, I accepted. If they were not offered, that was agreeable also. It is still in the Book that all things work together for good to them that love the Lord.

Practically all outside speaking engagements were made on my own time. As the area broadened to nearby towns, this became harder and harder, but The Evangel made it possible for me to fly to many places that I couldn't have made in an automobile and still keep up with the prison work.

Sometimes I even got lucky on the schedules and managed to sneak in a little recreation. The "Flying S Ranch" at Villa Rica, Georgia, had a good place to fish. One day I had some time to kill and dropped into the small airport. Everybody was away in town. I turned off the engine, went down to the lake and enjoyed some lazy fishing.

I thought there would be someone at the airport to help me take off, but there wasn't. Putting the chocks in front of the wheel, I cracked the throttle, turned on the magneto and then went out front to turn over the propeller. Any fool should have known better . . . but I didn't. The engine had been worked over two weeks before and was set up high. When it caught, I raced under the struts for the door . . . and didn't make it. The plane walked over the chocks and streaked down the strip. It may be a hard thing for people to believe, but the pilotless plane flew about three hundred feet, made a complete circle and landed where it had taken off. The torque of the engine (which produces rotation) made the plane circle. After the landing, it was the torque that drew the plane to one side of the airport. The craft ended up on its nose, with the propeller and a wheel knocked off.

A friend from Flightways flew down after I called him. He looked over the situation and then asked, "Are you injured?"

"No," I replied.

"You shouldn't be, because you weren't in it," he said, grinning.

"That's right. How did you know?"

"It was my business during the war to investigate planes that crashed."

An immediate problem arose as to how I could finance a re-rigging of the plane. God proved sufficient again. Two weeks before, a friend had asked me to take some downtown aerial photographs for business purposes. I was happy to help him. A few days after the crash, I received his check. It covered the damages, with a few dollars left over to cover the cost I had encountered in developing the pictures.

The rugged Evangel was like a faithful friend for nine years—and then came the day of her last flight. The Rotary Club of Thomson, Georgia, invited me for a speaking engagement, and the young man who telephoned the invitation said there was a vacant field where I could land. He sent me a map so I could find it. In checking further, he found that the map had been revised and sent me another, but it didn't arrive in Atlanta until after I had departed.

An Atlanta youngster interested in flying was with me on the flight. After two hours of flying southeast, we came to the designated field. The grass was five feet high and much too dangerous looking for a light plane.

Across the way was a large tower used by forestry men. Alongside was a little strip of clear space. In approaching I skimmed a house and fence, but landed safely, stopping near the highway. A car stopped on the road and the youngster crawled out. I yelled at the motorist, asking the location of the airport or a suitable field. He said an airport was nearby and pointed out the direction. I told my young friend to ride over with the motorist while I flew the plane out. The take-off was successful, but I was too late in seeing something that almost cost my life. Two small wires ran from a telegraph pole to the tower at a forty-five-degree angle. The ship shuddered when it hit them. Tips of the propeller were cut off and the wires went under the fuselage and attached themselves to the tail. There I was . . . like a boy's kite. The telephone company later figured that I stripped off one mile of telephone wire. Instinct told me to try to gain altitude, but common sense said to land quickly. I trimmed the ship and landed in the field on the other side of the highway. It was a rough mess in a rough field. A quick check disclosed a broken propeller, broken windshield, sheared left wing and fouled-up landing gear.

I stood there, sick inside about the faithful Evangel but feeling like the cat near the end of his nine lives. There were things to be done, however. The motorist was still waiting on the highway in his big Cadillac. I found out later he was the biggest "moonshiner" and liquor trafficker in the county, but he was nice and rushed me into town for the speaking engagement.

Thirty minutes after the ship had gone onto its nose, I was standing before almost a hundred men at the Thomson Rotary Club. In all the messages I have ever given, God gave me more strength that time. The president said that in his sixteen years as a Rotarian he had never heard such a talk.

I could only reply, "Sir, you have just heard a man who was almost ushered out into eternity less than an hour ago."

On the way back out to the plane, I placed the big problem in God's hands. He handled it well. A mechanic from the airport gave me $200 for the remains. Members of the Rotary Club made up $200 and sent it to me. The $400, however, fell far short of enough to put me in the airplane-riding business again. And the fund hasn't grown appreciably up to the time of this writing. I am still going to speaking engagements in an automobile.

The good ship Evangel, when last I heard, was being used at the Augusta Airport as a commercial plane for training.

HOME AND HOLLYWOOD

MARGARET AND I have tried to make our
home life as lovely and livable as possible. We have seen
the tragic results of so many broken homes that it
has almost become a phobia to guard ours, with God's
grace.

It hasn't been easy to find time for the people I love
best, with the prison work and outside speaking engagements, but such important things are rarely easy.
I take time to be with my family.

When the occasion calls for seriousness, we are
serious, but there is nothing mystic or pious about
the Tucker home. There's a lot of laughter in our
lives. Sometimes, however, Margaret doesn't think it

161

very funny when I joke about her following me from Wheaton to Houghton.

One of my hobbies has helped us grow close as a family. Great lessons in patience have been learned while carving on a piece of wood. And good thinking just comes naturally as the chips and minutes fall away.

The woodcarvers form a unique group in the United States. I became interested when I noted the beneficial effects the practice had on one of my parishioners in Ohio. To combat a health problem, doctors had prescribed using her hands on some hobby as an outlet for energy. She became a soap carver, and discovered a real talent. Some of her sculptures in soap were amazing.

As she became even more proficient and needed new worlds to conquer, she began whittling with a knife. Soon she was a master. Now a visiting professor at Marshall College in Huntington, West Virginia, she gives lectures on wood carving.

I thought such a hobby would be impossible for me, because of only one hand, but she thought otherwise and taught me many things. Improvement came steadily. Today my home is filled with carvings of horses, giraffes, dogs and many other creatures, along with lots of sawdust and shavings. There is even a stagecoach and four horses. Friends in Washington, D. C., London and many parts of the United States have other displays.

The hobby keeps fresh my outlook on life. It gives me

a closeness to my children in the workshop. Many fathers are too busy for such things. Carving also gives me relief from the intense activities and responsibilities of chaplain.

Margaret and I try to live the Christian life before our children. From the beginning, we have prayed for the children to know and love Jesus. If parents only could realize that a decision for Jesus is the greatest need in the lives of their children.

One Sunday night a few years ago, after a trying day and evening service I knew to be a total failure, I stood in front of the altar and gave an invitation for people to give their lives to Christ. There was no response, and I was about ready to give the benediction when a little seven-year-old girl stepped from the pews and walked down the aisle. She was my own flesh and blood—my daughter, Lynelle. I was all choked up as I looked down at the daughter for whom I had prayed even before she was born.

She said, "Daddy, I want to be a Christian. I want to give my heart to God."

Of all my experiences in the Christian faith, this was one of the greatest. God had allowed me to be the ambassador of the Lord to my own child. Lynelle reads her Bible and prays. They aren't memorized prayers. She prays from the heart—for her father, mother and brother, Richard, plus all the inmates in the penitentiary.

When God starts pouring out blessings, He seemingly

doesn't know when to quit. I thought everything possible had already happened, but the Lord was just getting warmed up when 1956 came around.

Things were going along smoothly at the prison and in our home, but Margaret was having quite a trial. She did an admirable job of keeping the surface unruffled, but she had a secret. She was a little jumpy. I put this down to the fact that I may have left too many wood carvings on the floor.

In looking back, I don't know how she was able to keep it. She is a woman and it was a big secret.

I found out what it was on a trip to California, where I had been invited to see a documentary film on "Criminal Rehabilitation."

The date was March 21, 1956. During the day I had toured one of our big prisons, and it was seven o'clock in the evening when I fidgeted in the corridor outside an NBC studio, waiting to see the documentary film.

Suddenly the corridor lit up like a Christmas tree, only more so, and a man stuck out his hand. He said, "Hello, Reverend Tucker, I'm Ralph Edwards. The lights that have come on signal the fact that you are being seen coast-to-coast on NBC television . . . Chaplain H. Park Tucker, This Is Your Life.

". . . if I said that you've lived twice, that you have two stories, the man you were and the man you've become, would I be right? Tonight, we're going to re-live with you a terrifying experience . . . when the man you were died and a new person was born. We're eager to know both of those fellows."

God gave me the grace not to be nervous or scared. Ralph made it easy, with his genuine friendliness. And he was the same way when the camera wasn't turning. He was wonderful, but the girl doing the commercial was prettier.

One of the nicest things about the program was that I had a chance to greet some of my congregation back in Atlanta. A limited number of the men are allowed to see the program each week.

Ralph continued his account of my life and then I heard a voice in the background, saying, "It is a surprising fact that at the Atlanta Penitentiary our average church attendance is larger than it is outside prison."

The exchange went something like this:

Ralph Edwards—"It's the big boss himself, here from Washington, D. C. He is the director of the U. S. Bureau of Prisons, Mr. James V. Bennett. Do you attribute this high church attendance to Chaplain Tucker, Mr. Bennett?"

Mr. Bennett—"Indeed I do. No prisoner is made to go to church. They turn out in such numbers because of Chaplain Tucker's own inspirational life, and his message. Some even give up stockade on Thursday to help him out."

Ralph Edwards—"What do you mean by stockade?"

Mr. Bennett—"Stockade is a period of games and exercise outside in the yard. The men prize this more than anything else. Many men often give this up to practice in Chaplain Tucker's choir.

"I think what the men really like about Chaplain

Tucker is that they know he's a 'square Joe' and will go to bat for those who are sincere. When tension is high, we look to men like Chaplain Tucker to help find the reason. We know the men trust him, and he will not betray their confidence."

Ralph Edwards—"Our congratulations to you, Mr. Bennett, and the Federal Bureau of Prisons. Your full-scale program of business courses, trade schools, psychotherapy and religion gives the prisoner every chance to return successfully to a new law-abiding society.

"Now, Chaplain Tucker, we have more surprises for you. Here is your wife, your daughter, Lynelle, and your son, Richard. Your family and friends have been staying at the Knickerbocker Hotel. There'll be a party for all of you there tonight."

Ralph presented Margaret and me with a movie projector, a gold charm bracelet and high fidelity phonograph, with built-in tape recorder.

And then he added some words that thrilled our souls:

"It has also been a heartfelt wish of yours to have a scholarship fund named in memory of your parents, so for the Joseph and Henrietta Tucker Scholarship Fund at Houghton College, we present you with this check for $1,000.

"This is your life, Chaplain H. Park Tucker. You rose above your handicap. You have become a force for mending lives. Your gifts of understanding and mercy have restored many men to decency and self-respect."

To all of this, I can only say, "To God be the glory, great things He hath done."

We had a wonderful time at the party. Margaret told me that keeping the secret was about the hardest thing she ever did. She had spent a lot of time on long distance telephone calls, giving information to the writers in Hollywood. And all of the calls had to be arranged for times when I would be away from home.

If a person discovers as little as five minutes before the program goes on the air that he is to be honor guest, his appearance will be cancelled and a film substituted. Edwards was so cautious that he arranged for Margaret and the children to take a different plane route to California from the one I followed. He didn't want any chance encounters.

The narrowest squeak came at the prison I visited during the day. Officials there, who knew I was to be on the program, thought I had left the premises for the studio and announced it so personnel could listen that evening. I was still in the prison, but found out later that I just happened to be in a section where the message was not given.

Before returning to Atlanta, we had a wonderful time showing the children some of the marvels of California. Highlights included Knott's Berry Farm and Calico City, California, a pleasure park. We enjoyed the re-enactment of the old Wild West, when, a hundred years ago, an average of ten men were killed on the streets of Calico every Saturday night.

167

After our return to Atlanta, we received many letters and telegrams from people all over the nation who had seen the television program. In scores of cases, they were letters of thanksgiving to God for the work He was doing in reclaiming the lives of prisoners.

Other letters were filled with questions about the fate of men after leaving the penitentiary. "Where do they go?" asked the people.

The same question has been asked thousands of times before. We know about those who return to prison. We see plenty of headlines about ex-convicts and parolees in new trouble. But what about those of whom we read nothing?

The following letter may answer the question:

Dear Reverend Tucker:

Your appearance tonight on "This Is Your Life" reminded me of something that I should have done many years ago.

In 1917 I was sentenced to the federal prison at Atlanta for an eight-year term. I was very young and while I was not a bad boy as boys go, I seemed never to be able to keep out of trouble. My childhood had been blighted by the loss of my father when I was but six years old. Lacking parental supervision, I wandered into a life of uselessness and crime.

But for such a man as you and some other interested persons, no telling where I might have wound up. I left the prison in 1919 after serving two years of my sentence and came back to my home state. Things were not easy for me here for I was from a small town, and of course everyone had heard of my troubles.

There were few who sympathized. I was lucky in finding

a very wonderful school chum who seemed to understand and wanted to help me in a new start. He took me in and taught me the decorating trade from top to bottom. Eventually I opened my own shop and for over thirty years have operated my own business here.

I married a very wonderful girl and we have raised a family of five boys and three girls, who are all married now and raising families of their own. The thirteenth grandchild was born yesterday to one of our daughters. I am loved and respected in our community and, while my record has been a disadvantage in some of the things that I could have done, I have never let it get me down. People have long since forgotten what I did. In spite of all they have given me positions of honor and trust for which I am very grateful.

My thought in writing you this letter was, that maybe some other boy would be inspired by my experiences to go the right way. Through experience I have learned the value of a good life. I know how hard it is alone, and a helping hand can mean the difference between success and failure.

In closing, may I leave this thought with you. Yours is a wonderful work for which there is little compensation save for the satisfaction and happiness you find in doing God's work. May God bless you and yours generously and make your hands and heart strong for there are too few to share the burdens of those who are weary and heartsick.

Such a man as this will never return to prison. Neither will thousands of others who have discovered the truth, ". . . if any man be in Christ, he is a new creature: old things are passed away; behold, all things are become new."

A CHAPLAIN NAMED JOHN

It would seem that nothing could top the incredible Hollywood experience. That should have been the climax to everything. But God doesn't often work according to human figuring. He used Hollywood as the springboard to opportunities of service beyond my greatest dreams.

Somewhere, sometime, I had heard these words: "No man ever stands so straight as he who stoops to help a boy." They had burned into my heart. But I had been so busy working among the adult results of sin that I had never had a real chance to get on the prevention level among red-blooded American boys. My prison parish was filled with men, many of whom had never had a chance.

One day I received an invitation from the southern jurisdictional director of the Boys' Clubs of America to make a speech in Phenix City, Alabama. Phenix City, I knew about. It was the sin city of the United States before National Guardsmen cleaned it out with martial law. We had always had a number of men from there in our institution. They had been tangled up in everything from the major leagues of gambling murders to taking young women across the state line for immoral purposes. The biggest crime of Phenix City, however, was the systematic looting of soldiers from nearby Fort Benning by well-dressed thugs and girls from throughout the United States, who made the city their headquarters. Comparatively few people from Alabama were involved.

I knew the meeting was to be for or about boys, and thanked God for it, but had no idea it would be anything but a routine get-together. I walked in and saw a lot of high-ranking officers from Fort Benning. A number of prominent people from Phenix City and nearby Columbus, Georgia, were present. Columbus and Phenix City are divided by a river.

Before I went to the podium, the director said:

"The purpose of this meeting is that we are trying to organize a Boys' Club in Phenix City, and we hope to get an option of purchase for the building that housed famous Club 714."

It was near this notorious establishment that Mr. Patterson, the late Attorney General of Alabama, was shot to death. The murder touched off all the public indignation that had been building up over the years under a cover of fear.

It inspired me to think of Club 714, a place where parasites had sapped the life-blood out of American soldiers, and to know that it might become a boys' club.

There was nothing fancy about the talk I gave to these influential men, who had it within their means to purchase several clubs for boys. It was simple, but I asked God to breathe upon every word. I began by recommending the thought of the man who "stands so straight" and asked that it be their motto.

The address, if it could be called that, went something like this:

"If you don't stoop down to lift them up today, I'll see them in the penitentiary tomorrow. They can be responsible businessmen and citizens, if you care enough to give them some love, some practical help, some sincere guidance. It's got to be from the heart. You can't fool a boy.

"I want to tell you the story of Leon Czolgoz. His is one of the stories of infamy in the United States. Quite a few years ago Leon Czolgoz' father was a respected businessman. But he never had time for his boy. Leon began going around with girls when he was fourteen or fifteen and caught one of the social diseases. At eighteen he married a beautiful high-school girl. A year later he was looking down at his wife in a hospital when she died in childbirth. Before leaving, he looked at his infant boy, an imbecile. Leon went behind the hospital and blew his brains out.

"The child grew up.

"President William McKinley visited Buffalo, New York, one day and tried to shake hands with as many people as possible. The child with a diseased brain pulled out a revolver and blew the President into eternity.

"A father didn't have time to muss his boy's hair or take him to a baseball game!

"Let's think about that boy of yours. He's quite a fellow, isn't he? I have a boy, too. He's nine years of age. I love him with all my heart. A great joy of my life is teaching and training him, and taking time to be with him as much as possible. All of us do important work—but, gentlemen, some things are more important than other things. Think about your boy twenty years from now. What is he going to be like?

"Earlier this year I took a little boat ride and visited the island of Alcatraz, a name feared by every criminal in America. The captain of the guard took me and two other men through A, B and C Cell Houses. Then he excused the other two men and took me into D Cell, the most infamous section of penology in the world. Some of the boys recognized me when I entered.

" 'Here comes that ——— preacher from Georgia,' one shouted.

"With an attempt at a sense of humor, I held up my hand. 'Peace, brethren, I thought I had rehabilitated you.'

"After the visit to D Cell, I was taken to a solitary confinement cell. There I looked upon an individual who will always give me the grace to fight for any group of boys. The man had been in solitary confinement for forty-seven years. Here was a life that had been totally wasted. He was in solitary confinement when horse and buggies outnumbered cars in the United States. He was in solitary confinement when Lindbergh flew across the ocean. He was in solitary confinement before American doughboys fought through the trench warfare of France in World War I. He was in solitary confinement when Bobby Jones won every major golf title, when Jack Dempsey was the greatest fighting man in the world, when Babe Ruth knocked sixty home runs out of major league parks.

"How much of your life would you have missed if you had been locked up in a cell for the last forty-seven years?

"The Bird-Man of Alcatraz, as he is known, would have had a different life if some person had cared enough to stoop down and lift him up when he was a boy. He might have become a brilliant diplomat, the president of a college, a minister, instead of the broken-down individual he is now. His sentence states that he shall be incarcerated in solitary confinement for the rest of his life.

"He came to Leavenworth Prison around the turn

of the century out of the Klondike in Alaska, one of our territories. He had killed a man in a brawl. At Leavenworth he was not receiving any mail and was bitter about it. To agitate him, a couple of inmates said, 'The reason you ain't receiving mail is that new officer, Mr. Turner, who was just transferred here from Atlanta. He's holding up your mail.'

"The angry prisoner, seemingly without thinking, walked over and stabbed Mr. Turner to death. The officer never knew what happened to him.

"The inmate was sentenced to be hanged. Then it was commuted to a life sentence in solitary confinement.

"God gave the Bird-Man plenty of intelligence, but he used little sense. He's an authority on canaries. That's where he got his nickname. He has studied canaries in his cell, dissected them, drawn pictures and diagrams of them and has even written a book about the birds. He has corresponded with many people throughout the nation about them.

"If he had a poor, diseased mind, there might be some excuse for his wasted life. But God gave him brains. I wonder how many men, when he was a boy, had an opportunity to show him some compassion and passed it by?

"A few weeks ago I had the unpleasant duty of burying one of our old inmates at Atlanta. He had entered the prison in 1911. When I met him about ten years ago he was so hard and crusted over that he would never attend church. He had nothing good to say for the minister, the Bible, or anything spiritual. When he died the friends he had were few. With a heavy heart, I preached his funeral. We took him out—the back door of parole, the inmates say—and placed his body in "Boot Hill." He was the 177th man to be placed there in the last fifty-five years.

"When it comes to the last mile, it is always the minister or the chaplain that is close to them. Ten dollars worth of flowers were put on his casket and he was given a Christian burial.

"I wonder who failed to give him a helping hand when it would have done some good?

"I am forty-seven years of age. And I am thinking of another man who would have been forty-seven years old if he had lived. He didn't live in Georgia, or Pennsylvania, or Maine. He came from a little town outside of Evansville, Indiana. When he was born, his mother almost died in the delivery. The father stood there at the bedside and looked at the tiny baby. She looked up, with her heart overflowing with the love that only a mother can possess, and asked, 'What shall we call the boy?' The husband said, 'Let's call him after that man of the Bible by the name of John.'

"The child was christened 'John.' John, like Park Tucker, had a good home. He went to school and had all the opportunities. Like Park Tucker, he was dismissed from school. He was reinstated, only to be dismissed again. He got a job and began to cheat at gambling. He was an expert at putting the eight ball in the side pocket. The law caught up with some of his

---

A CHAPLAIN NAMED JOHN

shady activities and he became an inmate of **Pendleton** State Penitentiary in Indiana. One night, with a razor blade and a piece of plywood, he carved an excellent replica of a revolver and shined it with shoe polish. When the guard came along he jabbed the toy gun into his ribs and whispered, 'Open the grating or I'll blow your head off.' The guard knew he was capable of anything and opened up. John invited a number of other prisoners to go along. They escaped into the night.

"For the next two years he was the most-wanted man in America by the Federal Bureau of Investigation. He spread a reign of terror wherever he went. Banks felt the fury of his guns. He was king of crime. To many people in the United States, he was actually a hero. The FBI dogged his trail and spread dragnets, but John always ducked out or shot his way through.

"The officers closed in again one dark, rainy Sunday night in Chicago at a theater, located across the street from McCormick Theological Seminary of the Presbyterian Church. The people there, most likely, were singing hymns and worshiping the Lord.

"The widely publicized 'woman in red' had tipped the officers. She put the finger on the man (who had changed his appearance with a face-lifting job) as he left the theater. When he started across the street, an FBI agent, with drawn revolver, moved up and said, 'John, if you move you'll die; you're under arrest.' John took his arm away from the arm of the girl. It seemed as if he were going to give up and fold his arms, but his hand streaked for an underarm holster.

"That was the last thing he ever did on earth!

"One bullet went through the base of the brain and out through his eye. Another slashed through his chin and out the top of his head. He fell in the dirty water of a Chicago street and died like a dog.

"Go to the thirteenth floor of the FBI headquarters in Washington, D. C., some day. You will be escorted into the room that is dedicated to this man of infamy. In the room you will see the death mask, where the shells went through his head. You'll see his broken glasses and his straw hat. You will see the steel vest that kept bullets from penetrating his body. His suit looks as if it has rust on it, but that's John's life's blood that flowed down over his coat as he died.

"There is a large book, with many entries of all the horrible things he did against society.

"Wouldn't it have been a wonderful thing this evening, when the gentleman stood up to introduce me as your speaker, if he could have said: 'The man who will address you is a fine Christian, and it gives me great pleasure, ladies and gentlemen, to introduce Chaplain John Dillinger of the United States Federal Penitentiary'?

"John Dillinger, the gangster, could have stood here if some man had cared enough to wage a loving fight for his soul. No man ever stooped so low.

"Many years ago, when I was a student in elementary school, I belonged to a Boy Scout troop. As a project, we had a famous speaker come to our church and commemorate a big holiday. He was William Jennings Bryan, the noted orator who ran for President of the United States.

"In trying to do my good deed for the day, I helped people find their seats, but whispered to my buddy, Gus, 'Go down to the front and spread out in two seats; one of them will be for me.' Gus did as he was asked, but in came old Granny Davis. She attended every service held in our church and always arrived late. I offered her this seat and that one, but she marched to the front, looked at Gus and said, 'Move over there, you got too much room.' She sat down in my seat.

"I stood there, looked at Granny Davis, looked at Gus, and was about to leave in resignation when I saw the kind face of a wonderful man. It belonged to William Jennings Bryan. With his keen perception he had discerned exactly what happened. He wiggled a finger and said, 'Come up here, son, I want to speak to you.'

"He smiled, 'That lady took your seat, didn't she? Well, you're going to have the best seat in the whole church. Jump up here and sit on my lap.'

"As long as I live I will never forget William Jennings Bryan. He put his arm around me and said, 'Some day, son, I hope you will be a real soldier for Christ.'

"This great Christian gentleman, who could have been excused if he had been more interested in his address than in an unknown boy, was kind to me and spoke a word for the Lord when he had an opportunity.

"Many years later, when I was a student at Wheaton Academy, he was still my hero and I remembered his prophetic words. One day, around October 1, my friends there staged a party. They walked into the room with a big package, opened it up and said, 'Park, here's your present.' It was a book, *The Life of William Jennings Bryan.*

"As I read chapter after chapter, and found again the warm arm of a gentleman as he showed a Boy Scout that somebody cared, it seemed exactly as if God's hand was upon me—just as it seems now, when I read the Bible, I can feel the arms of Jesus underneath it all, holding me up. One day I am going to meet Him face-to-face."

God spoke to the hearts of the businessmen that night in Phenix City. They contributed more than enough money, and the sign, "Boys' Clubs of America," now hangs over the entrance of Club 714. The roulette wheels aren't clicking inside. There are tools for boys to learn how to make things and games for them to play. A few shirts get dirty, but nobody loses them, as the GI's did in the games of no chance.

About a month later I was invited to attend the convention of Alabama and Georgia Boys' Clubs at Gainesville, Georgia. Scores of delegates from the two states met in a beautiful hotel. After my speech, the director asked if I would remain for a moment. He presented me with a citation and said, "This citation is the seventy-sixth to be given in the United States. The first one was given in January to President Eisenhower. One was given to each governor in the United States. You are now receiving the fiftieth gold medallion and citation to be given south of the Mason-Dixon line. The citation is for your work of inspiring and establishing a Boys' Club in Phenix City and for your work here at our convention."

Thank God for the time and opportunity to work among the boys of America. They are worth helping . . . so much!

AS I KNOW HIM

(In line with the age-old tradition of ladies
having the last word, I have asked my good
wife, Margaret, to write the last chapter of the
book. Here it is—uncensored.)

FROM THE BEGINNING, life with Park
Tucker has been comparable to living in a three-ring
circus.

It began at Wheaton College, when I was a homesick
freshman. It seemed as if Spring vacation would never
come. I counted the months, weeks, days and hours. The
real problem was a ride home, the cheaper the better,
money being what it was. I heard that a student named
Park Tucker had an old car and would be driving to
his family's home in Scranton, Pennsylvania.

His reply to my note was blunt—"Sorry, all filled." What a way to treat his future wife!

Our paths crossed only a few times during the year at Wheaton. I was a freshman in college. He was a senior in the Academy, a high school. We exchanged "hellos" occasionally in the dining hall, library and on the sidewalks. But he had eyes for only college seniors.

The country was in the throes of a depression. An aunt, for whom I was named, paid for my first year at Wheaton. Plans for a job the next year backfired, but the Great Architect knew what He was doing. Several days before school opened, arrangements were made for me to attend Houghton College in New York as a transfer student.

On the first day at Houghton, as I was walking by the Administration Building, I ran into Park Tucker. He often jokingly has accused me of following him to Houghton, but knows as well as I do that we arrived by different routes. He had read about it in Wheaton's library catalog section and I had heard of the school through an elder in our church. Houghton was nearer our homes, and expenses there were lower.

Mary, a young Bible student at the college, was an old friend of Park's. She and I became the best of friends and were dubbed the "blonde blizzards." Mary came from Wyoming, Pennsylvania, where her father was pastor of the Presbyterian Church.

Park made numerous trips around the countryside for testimony meetings. He had a 1936 Willys which ran on practically nothing. With money so scarce, this was a necessity, not a saving. One day, as a group of us were returning to Houghton from a Gospel-team excursion, there was a snort, bang, and then dead silence. The Willys rolled to a stop—out of gas! The engine had been running on its reputation for an hour.

There we were, stuck on a lonely road, with a strict deadline at the dormitory waiting for three worried girls. We pushed the car down the road and finally came to a gas station. There was no light inside. Park aroused the proprietor by persistent banging on the door. When he asked for only three gallons of gas, the man seemed to consider going back to bed. Then Park discovered that he had only thirty-seven cents. When he changed the order, the old man almost popped a blood vessel.

We didn't fall in love until Spring. As has been told in another part of this book, Park tricked me into my first utterance of "I love you." He knew I loved him, but I was reluctant to commit myself. He suggested spelling love. To this day, he is "LV" and I am "OE." It was a bit like the measles, however. Once I was broken out, I felt better.

Both of us worked while we were in school. Since Park had only one hand, he was the duster of the Science Building. Each morning it was his duty to dust all three floors of the building. One of the women professors doubted whether Park was cleaning her room each day and set a trap for him. She "planted" five dead flies. Park discovered the plot. Collecting the flies, he made five little caskets and placed them on her desk, with appropriate floral arrangements. There were no more traps!

One bitterly cold, snowy New York Sunday, Park spoke at a service in Industry, New York, where there was a penal colony. He gave his message, in the beginning, with little conviction. It was just another "assignment" from the school. During the talk he was convicted about his lack of real concern and silently asked the Lord for help. After completing the message, he asked the boys to give their hearts to God and to live for Christ.

There was no response, and Park thought the service a total failure. But our failures can be God's victories. A number of years later, while broadcasting from a Binghamton radio station, he gave the same invitation. After the service, a fine-looking man came into the station lobby and asked for Park. He introduced himself as an ex-inmate who had listened to the "dry" sermon at Industry and found the Lord. Later he took Park out to his farm for a visit with his wife and family. Perhaps this was an early glimpse God gave Park of his life's work.

One evening after study hall, Park and I were strolling back to the dormitory. He was wearing a pair of sad-looking white crepe-soled shoes given to him at a church in Warren, Pennsylvania. I told him they were a disgrace. He nonchalantly took them off and pitched them over the bank of the river. I was terribly embarrassed as my ex-coal-miner boy friend walked me home—barefooted.

Park and his studies had their eternal struggle. Chemistry and mathematics were difficult, but Greek was a monster. One day I waited for him to come out of Greek class with his examination paper. He was elated as he charged up to show me his "B." I looked it over, then had the unhappy chore of pointing out to him that the grade was "13," not "B."

An accident occurred at the end of one of our Gospel-team trips. One of the other boys had taken over the wheel from Park when a truck passed a car on a curve and sideswiped us. No one was seriously injured. The fellows asked the chief of police if they could stay in the local jail all night in order to be on hand and clear things up early next morning. Ken and Park were given a cell, but the gate wasn't locked. As he lay on the cot, Park didn't realize then that one day these people would be his parish.

I graduated in the class of '39. It was the end of a great struggle, but another one was about to begin.

Park was driving me home on the triumphant day and had covered sixty of the miles when he suddenly applied the brakes. He said he would have to return to school. His face was flushed, but intuition told me this was one of those times not to press my curiosity. When we got back he ran into the boarding house, came out with something and put it into the car trunk. Years later he confessed—he had forgotten his arm!

My rosy dreams for the future soon vanished in the light of reality. Teaching positions, when one could be found, paid $900 a year to start. I found employment selling jewelry in a large Philadelphia store.

When Park made his first appearance on the Chester scene, Dad was out front polishing the car. Park had an old briefcase under his arm and Dad mistook him for one of those fellows who went around collecting old gold. They were fairly common in those days. I happened to look out the door just in time to keep Park from being politely but firmly sent on his way.

During the next year, while Park was a senior, I visited Houghton only once, but he traveled 650 miles several times to see me. After graduation, he managed, with some difficulty, to gain admittance to Eastern Baptist Seminary in Philadelphia.

One day in class, dear old "Daddy" Maxwell shocked the students by announcing that his mother had two sons, one a preacher-teacher and the other a man who had spent most of his life in prison. Then he told the stunned students that his brother was a chaplain in the Lincoln, Nebraska, State Penitentiary. It was probably a stock joke with Dr. Maxwell, but the words "prison chaplain" started ringing in Park's subconscious.

During his first two years at the seminary, I taught at nearby Chester High School. It was a convenient arrangement. Then, in 1942, the great day came.

We were married and set up housekeeping in Ridley Park!

The apartment was small, so small in fact that Park declared half the furniture was painted on the walls.

187

I was the breadwinner. Park has often kidded about working his way through seminary on the sweat of his Frau.

These were war days. Many of Park's classmates were enlisting in the armed forces. Park tried, but they couldn't overlook his disability.

After graduation, it seemed logical that Park would accept a call from churches either in New Jersey or Pennsylvania. Along with my working, he could be a part-time pastor and take a war job in the bustling area. But God led differently. He sent us to a city we couldn't even spell—Chillicothe, Ohio.

We were to have many happy associations in Chillicothe, where Park was pastor of the Tabernacle Baptist Church. It was here that I gave birth to our daughter, Lynelle. While Park learned theology, I learned kneeology. Here we gave comfort through the Lord to the folks left behind when six gallant young men laid down their lives during the war. We had a vision that a new church should be built and helped raise the first $10,000. We met many friends, all of whom left their imprint on our lives and helped in our work for Christ.

Park also became a pilot here. I fought him and the Lord about the flying, but they won out.

It was in Chillicothe that Park received his life vision. The Federal Reformatory was located on the outskirts. Many of the staff were members of our church. When God called him to the work, he entered training at the Reformatory under the chaplain. In time he received his verification and resigned at the church to "jump over his prison wall" at Ashland, Kentucky.

Our son, Richard, was born during this tour of duty. Shortly after his birth, we left for the transfer to Atlanta. I was to drive the car we had finally acquired and Park was to fly in "The Evangel." He had an emergency landing and I had to stop while Lynelle broke out in beautiful red measles.

All of us finally made it, however, and for the last nine years we have lived within a stone's throw of the thirty-eight-foot wall that surrounds the Federal Penitentiary.

As a chaplain's wife, life is much different from that of a pastor's wife. I have been inside my husband's famous "church" only twice—once for an X ray when we thought Lynelle had swallowed a pin, and once as a visitor when the congregation honored the twelfth graduation of the Bible course written by Park.

I try to be a kind of buffer for the pressure the outside world puts on a man like Park. He is in great demand as a speaker. Another little task, I might add, is to pick up all the wood chips scattered throughout the house when Park is engaged in his hobby of whittling. But a house is not a home unless it is lived in. Take my word for it—Park, Lynelle and Dick do a lot of living.

Of course, I also take my active part in the community—president of the PTA, member of a choral group, Girl Scout leader, neighborhood chairman of the March of Dimes, welfare chairman of the prison women's auxiliary, superintendent and teacher in Sunday school, private tutor to my daughter in Milton Avenue School and son at Georgia Military Academy.

All these are my duties—and I love them.

Probably the biggest test of my life came when, for three months, I had to keep the secret that my husband was to be the subject in Hollywood on Ralph Edwards' "This Is Your Life" television program.

I knew that the program would be cancelled if I allowed Park to find out my secret. It was nerve-wracking. When I first talked over long distance with the writer assigned to the story, there were thirteen Brownie Girl Scouts running through every room in the house.

The writer and I worked out a schedule for telephone calls when Park was not supposed to be at home. But he upset the apple cart several times by being on hand when he was not supposed to be there. I had to sit by the phone on those days. He came in once while I was talking to Hollywood, but I escaped by saying, "I must hurry now; my husband is here and wants his dinner."

Everything finally worked out, but I was the most relieved person in California when the blinding studio lights went on and Mr. Edwards said: "Park Tucker, this is your life!"

Countless people are interested in having their life story told to the world. Thousands apply to Mr. Edwards and his staff every week. (We found out that Park was recommended by a friend at Emory University in Atlanta.) I believe God brought it all about because this was a story He wanted to be told—the story of miner 602, student, pilot, teacher, minister and prison chaplain, the story of a man who is devoting his life so others may hear the voice of God as He says "This Is Your Life; Enter into the Fold."

Park has received many honors since the Hollywood experience. All credit must go to the Lord. The honors were His doing and they were marvelous in our eyes. I was proud of each one, but my proudest day came in the Fall of 1956 when we went back to our old college, Houghton. Park was presented with an honorary doctor's degree. As the cowl was placed over his head, I bowed and thanked God for all His great goodness. I could appreciate more than others some of the memories that rushed through Park's mind in that sacred, wonderful moment, as he was honored by the college where he had once worked as a dust boy.

How can Park and I ever doubt God's simple question in the Bible—"Is any thing too hard for the Lord?"

Date Due